Universalism is a dangerous and malicious lie. It l[...]
you believe, sin is not really a problem, and ther[...]
single-handedly destroyed Christianity in much [...]
to destroy the faith of remnant believers in the .[...]
wholly different from the true God revealed in the Bible, Young mocks the importance and uniqueness of the Word of God. He makes the Bible equal to or less than whatever personal imagination anyone might have of God.

Dr. Michael Youssef
Leading the Way; Pastor, The Church of the Apostles

De Young's research on the biblical doctrines concerning humanity, God, and salvation is impeccable. His careful and detailed refutation of Paul Young's teachings serves as a much-needed correction for twenty-first-century pop theology.

J. Carl Laney
Professor of Biblical Literature, Western Seminary, Portland, OR

Paul Young, author of *Lies We Believe about God*, has produced a book whose misrepresentations of the words and teachings of Jesus are more blatant than those which surfaced in *The Shack*. Thankfully in this book, *EXPOSING "Lies We Believe About God"*, James B. De Young gives a thorough biblical critique of Paul Young's diatribe against Christianity. Paul Young has an appealing writing style, and his rhetoric sometimes grips the younger generations. With a Bible in your hand and the assistance of James De Young, you will emerge unscathed from an unprecedented threat to the faith of Jesus the Christ.

Paige Patterson
President, Southwestern Baptist Theological Seminary, Fort Worth, TX

From his personal acquaintance with Paul Young and his years of biblical teaching, James De Young writes a strong and thorough refutation of Young's attack on the core of Christian teaching. In each chapter, he responds from the Bible to Young's *Lies,* and in his appendices, he shows why Young cannot be considered orthodox. Read De Young's book to review the major points of evangelical faith.

John Van Diest
Publisher of Christian books

It is normally easier to discern what an author actually believes when the genre employed is non-fiction rather than a novel. Dr. De Young here takes advantage of that kind of shift in Paul Young's latest book to continue his much-needed warning about the nature and ramifications of Young's theology. In a systematic and thorough manner, De Young traces Young's multiple deviations from biblical orthodoxy and models a much more even-handed handling of Scripture.

Dr. Randal Roberts
President/Professor of Biblical Spirituality, Western Seminary, Portland, OR

Dr. James De Young has written a biblically saturated rebuttal to the insidious writings of Paul Young regarding *universal reconciliation* – a Satanically inspired, yet dangerously appealing, false teaching that trivializes life and death issues. Reading this book will illuminate the truth about the heretical nature of universal reconciliation, as well as strongly affirm the orthodox belief that eternal life is experienced through faith in the saving work of Jesus Christ alone.

Richard Malcolm, ThM
A former student and colleague of De Young's

The prophet Jeremiah warned the Babylonian captives to watch out for the wolves among them. That warning still applies today. Thanks to wise and discerning men like James De Young, the Church is being warned *not* to believe half-truths wrapped around the shoddy doctrines of "another gospel" and heretical teachings that can so easily lead people away from Calvary. This book is a wake-up call to the Church in the twenty-first century. It is a must read!

Janet Parshall
National radio host, speaker, and author; Host/Executive Producer, "In The Market"

James De Young made an impact on my radio audience about the time *The Shack* film came out. He knows, perhaps better than anyone, the stealth attack Paul Young has perpetrated on Christians. Listen to his warnings in this new book.

Jan Markell
Founder/Director, Olive Tree Ministries

In *Lies We Believe about God*, Wm. Paul Young is proposing truth about God; the title itself declares this intent. Any professing Christian should respond to this as did the Berean believers upon hearing the proclamations of Paul in Acts 17:11. They *examined the Scriptures every day to see if what Paul said was true*. In EXPOSING *"Lies We Believe About God"*, James De Young has initiated that process for those who read Young and desire to know the truth. Read it prayerfully with your Bible open and with your heart ready to know and submit to the God of truth.

Steven Hardy
Pastor, Damascus Community Church

James B. De Young has given the church a masterful biblical refutation of the latest book from popular author Paul Young, whose embrace of universal reconciliation has influenced millions of evangelicals. With Scriptural clarity and discernment, De Young breaks down the lies of the man whose real goal is to change Christianity. A marvelous exposé that needs to be widely read!

Janet Mefferd
Nationally syndicated Christian radio host

When *The Shack* was published, William Paul Young was asked if he believed in universal salvation, and he adamantly denied that his book promoted universalism. But now, ten years later, he openly admits it. As an acquaintance of William Paul Young, James B. De Young is more than qualified to refute Paul Young's latest book, *Lies We Believe about God*. This is a must-read for those who are contending for the faith in these last days, as it will better equip you to be a defender of the truth, in light of the apostle Paul's warning about those who would preach "another gospel."

Dwight Douville
Senior Pastor, Calvary Chapel of Appleton, WI

I am pleased to heartily recommend Dr. James B. De Young's new book, *EXPOSING "Lies We Believe About God"*. Now that Paul Young has stepped out from behind the characters in his novels to more directly reveal his theology and intent, Dr. De Young's latest book focuses with absolute clarity on the core issues that every biblically minded Christian needs to be aware of. I pray each reader will read and accept EXPOSING *"Lies We Believe About God"* as a God-sent warning about false teaching rooted inside Christendom in these last days.

Eric Barger
Founder, Take A Stand! Ministries and author of *Disarming the Powers of Darkness*

Sometimes the best way to love others is to tell them the truth. In *EXPOSING "Lies We Believe About God"*, James De Young does just that. Exposing error in defense of the truth is becoming increasingly necessary in a world of self-appointed authorities. Read this book and the one being challenged with the sword of the Spirit between them; then make your decision about which best represents the truth. It won't be hard to tell.

Mark L. Bailey
President, Dallas Theological Seminary

With clarity and conviction, in fairness and in a now-strained friendship, Dr. James DeYoung presents the lies, distortions and straw-man arguments that celebrated novelist Paul Young asserts in his troubling book. In turning from evangelical faith to Universalism and propagating his heresy to many, Young has become an "evangelist of a bad gospel." James DeYoung's powerful critique is needed and welcome.

Dr. Ronald B. Allen
Senior Professor of Bible Exposition, Dallas Theological Seminary

EXPOSING
"Lies We Believe About God"

How the Author of *The Shack*
Is Deceiving Millions of Christians
Again

James B. De Young, Th.D.

EXPOSING "Lies We Believe About God" – James B. De Young, Th.D.

Copyright © 2018

First edition published 2017

Cover Design: J. Martin

eBook Icon: Icons Vector/Shutterstock

Editors: Sheila Wilkinson and Paul Miller

Printed in the United States of America

Aneko Press

www.anekopress.com

Aneko Press, Life Sentence Publishing, and our logos are trademarks of

Life Sentence Publishing, Inc.
203 E. Birch Street
P.O. Box 652
Abbotsford, WI 54405

RELIGION / Christian Theology / Apologetics

Paperback ISBN: 978-1-62245-603-1

eBook ISBN: 978-1-62245-604-8

10 9 8 7 6 5 4 3 2 1

Available where books are sold

Contents

PREFACE

The Scriptures (both the prophets and the apostles) clearly warn about false teaching.

Jeremiah 23:26-28, 32: *How long shall there be lies in the heart of the prophets who prophesy lies, and who prophesy the deceit of their own heart, who think to make my people forget my name by their dreams that they tell one another, even as their fathers forgot my name for Baal? Let the prophet who has a dream tell the dream, but let him who has my word speak my word faithfully. What has straw in common with wheat? declares the LORD.*

Behold, I am against those who prophesy lying dreams, declares the LORD, who tell them and lead my people astray by their lies and their recklessness, when I did not send them or charge them. So they do not profit this people at all, declares the LORD.

1 Timothy 4:16: *Keep a close watch on yourself and on the teaching. Persist in this, for by so doing you will save both yourself and your hearers.*

1 Timothy 6:3-5: *If anyone teaches a different doctrine and does not agree with the sound words of our Lord Jesus Christ and the teaching that accords with godliness, he is puffed up with conceit and understands nothing. He has an unhealthy craving for controversy and for quarrels about words, which produce envy, dissension, slander, evil suspicions, and constant friction among people who are depraved in mind and deprived of the truth, imagining that godliness is a means of gain.*

1 Timothy 6:20: *O Timothy, guard the deposit entrusted to you. Avoid the irreverent babble and contradictions of what is falsely called "knowledge," for by professing it some have swerved from the faith.*

2 Timothy 1:13-14: *Follow the pattern of the sound words that you have heard from me, in the faith and love that are in Christ Jesus. By the Holy Spirit who dwells within us, guard the good deposit entrusted to you.*

2 Timothy 3:13-17: *Evil people and imposters will go on from bad to worse, deceiving and being deceived. But as for you, continue in what you have learned and have firmly believed, knowing from whom you learned it and how from childhood you have been acquainted with the sacred writings, which are able to make you wise for salvation through faith in Christ Jesus. All Scripture is breathed out by God and profitable for teaching, for reproof, for correction, and for training in righteousness, that the man of God may be complete, equipped for every good work.*

2 Timothy 4:1-4: *I charge you in the presence of God and of Christ Jesus, who is to judge the living and the dead, and by his appearing and his kingdom: preach the word; be ready in season and out of season; reprove, rebuke, and exhort, with complete patience and teaching. For the time is coming when people will not endure sound teaching, but having itching ears they will accumulate for themselves teachers to suit their own passions, and will turn away from listening to the truth and wander off into myths.*

Titus 3:10: *As for a person who stirs up division, after warning him once and then twice, have nothing more to do with him, knowing that such a person is warped and sinful; he is self-condemned.*

Jude 24-25: *Now to him who is able to keep you from stumbling and to present you blameless before the presence of his glory with great joy, to the only God, our Savior, through Jesus Christ our Lord, be glory, majesty, power, and authority, before all time and now and forever. Amen.*

INTRODUCTION

The Author of *The Shack* Writes a New Book
Filled with Universalism/Heresy

Unless otherwise stated, all page numbers at the end of sentences are from *Lies We Believe about God,* referenced below.[1] Likewise, the first reference to *The Shack* will be footnoted, and after that only the title with page number will follow the sentence.

What would you think of a book written by someone who claims to be a Christian (57) and . . .

- Who believes that all people are "fundamentally good" and not sinners (35)?

- Who does not believe that God is in control of everything (42)?

- Who believes that God submits as much to our plans as we do to his (43)?

- Who redefines God's nature as a sexual being (93)?

- Who claims that the "feminine/masculine nature of God is a circle of relationship" in which all humans participate (73)?

- Who believes that the God of Christian faith is a "torture-devising" God (149)?

- Who claims that neither hell nor sin brings separation from God (134; 231)?

---

1   Wm. Paul Young, *Lies We Believe About God* (New York: Simon & Schuster, Inc., 2017).

- Who claims that the cross – the death of Christ – was not in God's plan, but was man's idea (149)?

- Who claims that the sacrifice of Christ on the cross was "cosmic abuse" of a child (149)?

- Who believes that unsaved people can still choose to turn to God after they die (185-186)?

- Who thinks that the institutions of the church, the government, and marriage are man-created and even demonic (103, 111-113; *The Shack*, 122-124, 179)?

- Who thinks that bearing a weapon and killing in war is murder (104-105)?

- Who claims that every human being is a child of God, already saved and reconciled to God (120)?

- Who claims that the evangelical Christian view of the Trinity embraces a distant deity who originated evil and whose plan included the torture of a child (238)?

- Who claims that the early church father Athanasius and the Nicene Creed support his beliefs (see appendices)?

You may ask, "Who would ever write such things?" You would guess that this is some obscure author who has virtually no impact on the Christian world. You would be wrong. The author is Wm. Paul Young, the most successful author of the last decade! His novel *The Shack*, along with his other novels, have sold over twenty million copies. *The Shack* has also been made into a Hollywood film.[2]

Yes, in his new book, Paul Young has made not only the preceding assertions but many more. His newest book is *Lies We Believe about God* (to be referred to as simply *Lies* from here on), released in early March 2017. *Lies* is about doctrine. It is not a fictional novel.

In this book, Young has twenty-eight brief chapters, with each chapter title being a "lie" that he believes is an erroneous belief of Christians, particularly evangelical Christians. Then he seeks to demolish each

---

2   Wm. Paul Young, *The Shack* (Newbury Park, CA: Windblown Media, 2007).

"lie" and show that each one is false. For support, Young sometimes appeals to the Bible, but more often he appeals to personal experiences.

Other Radical Theology from *Lies We Believe about God*

As if it weren't enough that Paul Young has provocative titles for his twenty-eight chapters, even more radical ideas are scattered within these chapters. Here is a sampling, seventeen in number. In many instances, Young first raises a question, and then answers it for us.

All people are "fundamentally good" because they were "created in Christ" (35).

"The Golden Rule is . . . the way God is. God treats me exactly the way God wants to be treated" (46).

"What is the incarnation – God becoming fully human – if not complete and utter submission to us? What about the cross, in which God submits to our anger, rage, and wrath?" (48).

"The image of God in us (*imago dei*) is not less feminine than masculine. The feminine/masculine nature of God is a circle of relationship, a spectrum, not a polarity" (73).

"Where do you think sexuality originates? It originates in the very being of God" (93).

"When the New Testament tells us that the divine nature of God has been placed within us, the Greek word used is *sperma*" (95).

"The Good News is *not* that Jesus has opened up the possibility of salvation and you have been invited to receive Jesus into your life. The Gospel is that Jesus has already included you into His life, into His relationship with God the Father, and into His anointing in the Holy Spirit. The Good News is that Jesus did this without your vote, and whether you believe it or not won't make it any less or more true" (117-118).

In answer to the questions, "Are you suggesting that everyone is saved? That you believe in universal salvation?" Young's answer is, "That is exactly what I am saying! This is real good news!" (118).

"Here's the truth: every person who has ever been conceived was included in the death, burial, resurrection, and ascension of Jesus" (119).

"We don't offer anyone what has already been given; we simply celebrate the Good News with each one: *We have all been included*" in salvation (120).

"Doesn't it seem intuitively wrong to be desperately afraid of a torture-devising God and yet hope to spend eternity with this God?" (132). Young continues, ". . . perhaps hell is hell not because of the absence of God, but because of the presence of God, the continuous and confrontational presence of fiery Love and Goodness and Freedom that intends to destroy every vestige of evil and darkness that prevents us from being fully free and fully alive" (136).

In reply to the question "Who originated the Cross?" Young replies, "If God did, then we worship a cosmic abuser, who in Divine Wisdom created a means to torture human beings in the most painful and abhorrent manner. . . . Better no god at all, than this one" (149).

Does belief in Love, Life, and Truth, even by an atheist, make him "a child of God? No, it doesn't. He already was a child of God" (205).

Young's definition of sin (Greek *hamartia*) is this: "Sin is anything that negates or diminishes or misrepresents the truth of who you are" (229).

If the idea that sin separates us from God "is a lie, does it mean that no one has ever been separated from God? That is exactly what it means" (232).

"Let me tell you about the God who actually showed up and healed my broken heart, not the god I grew up with in my modern evangelical Christian fundamentalism" (236).

"The God I grew up with was of little comfort. In fact, that God was considered the originator of evil, a distant deity who had a plan that included the torture of a child. One can't run to God if God is the perpetrator" (238).

The Tie that Binds

More statements like these fill Young's book, but these are among the most alarming in his confrontation with Christian belief.

Do you get the idea that Paul Young is out to change Christianity? You are exactly right, as Young himself admits (see below).

As I will show below, the belief that binds all twenty-eight chapters and their content together is universal reconciliation (UR). This belief is foundational to all of *Lies*. Young himself confesses his adherence to UR in chapter 13 of his book.

A Brief but Necessary Background

Why would Paul Young write such a book? The answer is that he became a convert to universal reconciliation prior to 2004 and is zealous to promote it. In that year, he presented a 103-page paper to a Christian forum that he and I co-founded in 1997. In this paper, he said he was rejecting his "evangelical paradigm" and embracing UR. He defended his new belief system by appealing to the teaching of the Bible, to reason and emotion, and to early church history. Young asserted that this new belief system transformed him and changed his life. It made him a more loving, open person, and it affected everything he believes about God, about doctrine, and about the Bible. When I responded the following month with a paper objecting to his paper, he was a no-show. He never attended our monthly forum again.

Out of his new belief system, Young wrote *The Shack* as a novel for his kids. He and two pastor friends spent a year removing the obvious universal reconciliation from the book, since the two pastors were bothered by the explicit UR. Then he and his friends self-published the second edition of the novel for adults. To date, the novel has sold multiple millions of copies.

Upon reading *The Shack,* I discovered that UR is deeply and subtly embedded in the novel. Because of my personal knowledge of what led to *The Shack* and its revision, I wrote *Burning Down "The Shack": How the "Christian" Bestseller Is Deceiving Millions* to expose this deception – deception, because Young has repeatedly denied that he is a universalist and claims that the book is fiction.[3] Yet he also claims that it is theological and autobiographical. I isolated twenty-one statements to show that UR is embedded in the novel.[4]

In March 2017, the film based on the novel appeared in theaters. This event has promoted the basic teaching of *The Shack* even further. Most of the twenty-one statements appear, in various ways, throughout the movie.

How do I explain the success of the novel and the film? I think that much of it is linked to Paul's personal testimony that he frequently seeks to promote in personal appearances and in interviews. From his own deeply flawed, broken, and tragic past, Young gains a great deal of sympathy. His success also feeds on the growing biblical ignorance and illiteracy among both non-Christians and Christians, even among pastors.

Other Novels by Paul Young Propagate Universal Reconciliation

In addition to *The Shack,* Young has published two other novels: *Cross Roads* (2012)[5] and *Eve* (2015).[6] In both of these, the basic UR is unmistakable and forms the foundation for Young's "novel ideas." For example, in chapter 13 of *Cross Roads,* Young has a dialogue in which

3   James De Young, *Burning Down the Shack* (Washington, D.C.: WorldNetDaily, 2010).
4   See the introduction to *Burning Down the Shack*, ix-x.
5   Wm. Paul Young, *Cross Roads* (London: Hodder & Stoughton Ltd, 2012).
6   Wm. Paul Young, *Eve* (New York: Howard Books, 2015).

the evangelical understanding of the judgment and the wrath of God is identified as "lies" eight times![7]

In *Eve*, Young has Adam already "turning away" (the words are Young's attempt to deal with Adam's fall into sin and rebellion) from God on the sixth day, before he names the animals (Genesis 2). He makes Adam the cause of Eve's and the serpent's "turning away." Adam is not created as an adult out of dust, but is born out of the womb of Christ (the "Eternal Man") as a baby (Genesis 2:7). Eve is conceived in Adam's womb and born as a baby. Both Adam and Eve are nursed at the breasts of Eternal Man! A mythological woman, Lilith, predominates in the novel.

I said that Young comes up with "novel ideas," but a better description is to say that he distorts the biblical account of Genesis chapters 1-3 almost beyond recognition. A most glaring example is his making Adam the cause for the sin of both Eve and the serpent, contrary to the Bible.

Why *Lies* Is So Important

The preceding brief account is necessary for readers of this response so they will understand why it is important to grasp what the newest book, *Lies*, is all about. In his book, Young openly and boldly confesses his adherence to universal reconciliation (118). When asked if he believes in universal reconciliation, he says, "That is exactly what I am saying!"

Lies is important from another standpoint – Young's truthfulness. On more than one occasion, Young has denied being a (general) universalist. In addition, he came to my home in 2008, after the publication of *The Shack*, and said before many witnesses, including my pastor, that he no longer believed in UR and wanted me to stop circulating his paper of 2004. But now in *Lies*, he confesses that he believes in UR and apparently has believed it all along for at least thirteen years. At last the cat is out of the bag.

When Young recounts the writing of *The Shack*, as he does most fully in chapter 28 of *Lies*, and also in interviews, why does he omit his open espousal of UR in the first writing of the novel for his kids? Why does he omit the fact that the novel people buy is really the second

---

7   Wm. Paul Young, *Cross Roads*.

edition? Why does he not reveal what the first edition contained? Why does he not disclose the fact that his fellow editors of the second edition sued him in court, claiming that they, as co-authors, deserved a bigger share of the proceeds from the sales of the novel and the film? When he is asked in public appearances about his universalism, why has he not confessed his conversion to UR?

Lies is also significant for the influence that it will have on the beliefs of so many people. With his several novels selling millions of copies, this book is also bound to sell well just by virtue of being by Wm. Paul Young. If he were not the author, I think that most Christians would consider his book, *Lies*, to be an oddity by a wayward, pseudo-Christian writer.

The author and his friends certainly consider this book important. They think that Young could be the biggest writer of the past five hundred years.

C. Baxter Kruger, who wrote the foreword for *Lies*, thinks so. On his website, Kruger makes statements lauding the work of Paul Young in his post "The Genius of *The Shack*."[8] He remarks that Young is presenting "a large-scale challenge of Western Christianity." He is challenging our "religious inheritance" and our "fundamental notions of God," which have "misled us." Who, he asks, is willing to "get down to the serious work of reformation"? He continues: ". . . the religious and personal challenges are not going to go away. Thank God. As Luther unwittingly started a revolution when he nailed his theses to the Wittenberg door, Paul Young may well have done the same when he wrote a little story for his kids. We will see."

Why would Young release *Lies* at this time? With the success of his novels, he probably believes that his following is great enough that this confession will not blemish his reputation and that it will enhance the growth of UR. Young is on a campaign looking for converts to UR. Lest anyone doubt this, they should note his comments in an interview conducted by *Religious News Service*.[9] He said the structures of the evangelical church are collapsing and new questions are being raised.

---

8   C. Baxter Kruger, "The Genius of *The Shack*," *Perichoresis: www.perichoresis.org/the-genius-of-the-shack/* (February 28, 2017; accessed May 31, 2017).

9   Emily McFarlan Miller, "Controversial Book *The Shack* Makes the Leap from Page to Screen," *Religious News Service: http://religionnews.com/2017/03/03/controversial-book-the-shack-makes-the-leap-from-page-to-screen/* (March 3, 2017; accessed May 31, 2017).

He said he stands on the "cusp of a new reformation," a work brought about by the Holy Spirit. Young is seeking to promote UR as the new, all-comprehensive theology for those seeking to know God.

The foregoing shows how serious Young and others view his writings. Those, like Young, who champion UR, pose the greatest threat to the evangelical church in two hundred years. I say this based on having studied the history of UR from the early church on and in early America.[10]

What Is Universal Reconciliation?

I've written about UR elsewhere (see my book, *Burning Down the Shack*, and my website: *burningdowntheshackbook.com*), but here is a brief history of UR and a succinct list of its tenets. It has been a thorn in the side of Christianity since the third century and was declared heretical in the sixth century.

The Need to Distinguish Universal Reconciliation from Other Forms

In summary, universal reconciliation (UR) is the Christian form of universalism, which insists that all people will be restored to God after a future "correction" in hell. Another form of universalism asserts that restoration takes place immediately after death. In its various forms, universalism goes back a long time. In America, it has a checkered history that began in the 1760s and 1770s. Several creeds were issued.[11]

In 1878, at Winchester, New Hampshire, the idea of restoration only after chastisement was declared by the Universalist movement in America to be the orthodox view. "Penitence, forgiveness, and regeneration" are all involved.[12] Earlier, due to the influence of the universalist Hosea Ballou, most universalists through much of the nineteenth century

---

10 I've completed a major manuscript on UR, to be published soon. It covers all the arguments of UR from the Bible, from emotion and reason, and from church history. From 1760 on, universalism grew rapidly in early America for a hundred years until Christian writers like Isaac Backus exposed its fallacies. Now with the writings of Young and others, universalism is experiencing a resurgence not seen for almost two hundred years.

11 You can read these creeds in appendix 3, "Creeds of Universalism," in my book, *Burning Down the Shack*.

12 Gerstner, "Universalism," *Baker's Dictionary of Theology*, ed. E. F. Harrison (Grand Rapids: Baker, 1966), 539. See the similar entry in the *Evangelical Dictionary of Theology*, ed. Walter A. Elwell (Grand Rapids: Baker, 1984, 2001).

were persuaded that hell did not exist for anyone after death, but only bliss. More recently, in 2007, the Christian Universalist Association was formed to separate universal reconciliation from Unitarian universalism.

There is also a pagan form of universalism – general universalism – that teaches that all will ultimately be happy, since all are by nature the creatures and children of God.[13] This view asserts that Jesus is just one of many ways to God or that all go to heaven because Christ's death covers all people's sins whether or not they have ever heard of Jesus Christ. In this book I am specifically focusing on universal reconciliation, which is what Young's writings are about, but much of what I write pertains to all forms of universalism.[14]

The Beliefs of Universal Reconciliation

So what is universalism – and in particular, what is universal reconciliation? The beliefs of universal reconciliation (UR) may be identified from the writings of its adherents, past and present. In strategic ways, universalism differs from evangelical faith. The following points are common to a more comprehensive definition and understanding of UR. They are the primary points by which one recognizes the language of universal reconciliation.

1. God wills all his created beings, both people and angels, to be saved and to acknowledge Jesus as Lord; and (this is important) God's will cannot be thwarted (Colossians 1:19-20; 1 Timothy 2:4).

2. God's attribute of love limits his attribute of justice. It is unjust

---

13   Ibid. See also M. Erickson, *Christian Theology*, 2nd ed. (Grand Rapids: Baker, 1998), 1026-1028, who cites other forms of universalism (universal conversion by evangelism, universal atonement, universal opportunity to respond) that are not examples of true universalism. In contrast to the classic form expressed by Origen, true universalism may take the forms of universal explicit opportunity (before or after death all place faith in Christ after explicitly hearing the gospel), universal reconciliation (reconciliation is already an accomplished fact for all), and universal pardon (in the end God will change his mind about condemning many and impute not only righteousness but also faith to all, and will forgive all). See also Erickson's discussion of universalism in William V. Crockett and James G. Sigountos, eds., *Through No Fault of Their Own? The Fate of Those Who Have Never Heard* (Grand Rapids: Baker, 1991), 23-33.

14   Thus, when I use the words "universalism" and "universalist," I have "universal reconciliation" primarily in mind. This wording is not meant to be lacking in precision, for I note that Young, McLaren, Bell, and others repeatedly use the broader term in their works. Paul Young's universalism seems to combine universal opportunity and universal reconciliation.

for a loving God to send people who have lived a short life to an eternal (everlasting) hell.

3. God has already reconciled all created beings – all humanity and all angels – to himself by the atonement of Jesus Christ at the cross.

4. This reconciliation will be applied to all people either before death or after death and to all the fallen angels, including the devil.

5. Faith is necessary to appropriate reconciliation in this life; God's love delivers unbelievers, fallen angels, and the devil from hell in the next life.

6. The sufferings of hell and the lake of fire are not punitive, penal, or eternal, but are purgatorial, corrective, restorative, purifying, cleansing, and limited in duration.

7. Hell and the lake of fire are not forever, but will cease to exist after all people and the fallen angels, including the devil, have been delivered from them and enter heaven.

8. God has acted as the judge of all at the cross; there is not a future judgment for anyone.

9. The work of the Holy Spirit is given little, if any, attention.

10. The work of Satan (the devil) is given little, if any, attention.

11. Universalism claims that its teachings are the teachings of the Bible – the teachings of Jesus.

12. Universalism claims that it was the majority belief of the Christian church for the first five centuries.

13. The evangelical church is an obstacle to universalism.

14. All institutions, including the church, marriage, and the government, are systems of hierarchy that use power to control people.

15. Universalists pride themselves on being independent of any creed. They insist that they should not be pinned down regarding their beliefs.

The chief argument of universalism is based on the emotional appeal to God's mercy and love, emphasizing that he could not bring everlasting suffering to any of his creatures. Universalists argue: How can a loving God torment billions of people forever in hell, the lake of fire, for failing to believe during a lifetime of a relatively few number of years?[15] God's justice is completely in the service of his love.[16] Universalists also appeal to Scripture (although this appeal is distorted) and to history (this appeal is also distorted), but in the end these claims take second place to the appeal to a sense of fairness and justice limited by God's love in his dealing with people. Universalists assert that God's love is his supreme attribute, and love and justice are mutually exclusive.

Young's Universalism

Paul Young has his own unique style of UR. He is even less Christian than many others. Here is a shorter list of what he believes, as derived from his writings, websites, and interviews. We can boil down the preceding into the primary teachings and distortions of his UR.

1. The God of the Old Testament is different from the Jesus of the New Testament.

2. Love is the supreme attribute of God. Love limits God's other attributes.

3. All people are equally the children of God already because of his love. All are saved.

4. There is no everlasting punishment for sin, no lasting hell, because sin does not separate anyone from God. Even hell is not separation from God. Separation is redefined.

5. There is an incomplete picture of sin and evil. Sin is redefined.

6. God's justice is subjected to his love.

---

15   This argument is fallacious. See my document: "The Sledgehammer of Universalism" on my website, burningdowntheshackbook.com, where I show that just the opposite is true: more people will be in heaven than in hell.

16   Erickson, *Theology*, 1028, citing the universalist Nels Ferre, *The Christian Understanding of God* (New York: Harper & Brothers, 1951), 228. Ferre asserts that love and justice or punishment, heaven and hell, are mutually exclusive (237). Paul Young, Rob Bell, Brian McLaren and others are simply the most contemporary proponents of this argument.

7. The person of Jesus is distorted; he is the savior of all and the judge of none.

8. The nature of God is distorted; wrath and anger are not part of his nature or expressions of it. Judgment is redefined as mercy, and holiness is redefined as love.

9. Masculine/feminine sexuality belongs to the nature of God, and people are in a deep relationship with God as such, because they were created "in God."

10. Reconciliation of all people was accomplished at the cross without people exercising faith.

11. Faith is given scant attention. Young ridicules the categories of "believer" and "unbeliever."

12. There is no future judgment.

13. Death is not a barrier to anyone's changing his destiny from hell to heaven.

14. The institutions of marriage, the church, and government are diabolical. In *The Shack,* Young has Jesus say that they are a "trinity of terrors," and that he (Jesus) never created any of them.

15. Church history is distorted, so that it is read as supporting UR.

16. There is scorn for commitment to a system of belief (a creed).

In the following response to *Lies*, it will be evident that these concepts belonging to UR form the underpinning for everything in *Lies*.

In *Lies*, Young sets forth a systematic theology of sorts. This means that he addresses the span of topics covered in doctrinal teaching. A systematic theology covers the nature and person of God as a triune being. It includes the study of God the Father, God the Son, and God the Holy Spirit. It studies the nature of human beings, angels, fallen angels (including Satan), salvation, bibliology (the study of the Bible), sin, eschatology (the study of the end times), and other topics. As will be seen in the sections of this book, Paul Young covers almost all of these areas, some more extensively than others. One area seems to be unaddressed almost entirely, and that is eschatology, the doctrine about the end times and the return of Jesus Christ – as he promised his followers (John 14:1-3). This is the hope of all Christians.

Sample of Chapter Titles/Lies

Below is a list of some of the most important chapters and their titles – the "lies" that I am exposing. Young says that we evangelical Christians profess all of them.

Ch. 1. "God loves us, but doesn't like us." Young emphasizes the object of the love (us), not the Lover.

Ch. 3. "God is in control." Young claims that God is not in control of everything.

Ch. 4. "God does not submit." God does submit to human beings, Young says.

Ch. 5. "God is a Christian." The movie and the novel both have Jesus saying that he is not a Christian.

Ch. 7. "God is more he than she." Young asserts that in his *nature* – who he is – God is equally masculine and feminine.

Ch. 13. "You need to get saved." Young embraces "universal salvation." Everyone is already saved.

Ch. 15. "Hell is separation from God." No, Young says, hell does not separate anyone from God. God is in hell.

Ch. 17. "The Cross was God's idea." Young says it was man's idea; otherwise God is a "cosmic abuser."

Ch. 19. "God requires child sacrifice." The sacrifice of Jesus was not to satisfy God's righteousness, Young asserts.

Ch. 22. "God is not involved in my suffering." Young says that God infuses our suffering with Presence and Love.

Ch. 24. "Not everyone is a child of God." Young claims that everyone is a child of God.

Ch. 27. "Sin separates us from God." Young redefines sin. Sin does not separate us from God.

Ch. 28. "God is One alone." Young's understanding of the Trinity is not from his "evangelical Christian fundamentalism," which affirmed a "distant deity" involved in the "torture of a child."

Could Paul Young make it any clearer that he is not a Christian, that he is not an evangelical? At last the genie is out of the bottle.

Other Things First: What the Foreword and Introduction to *Lies* Reveal

Before I get to the substance of *Lies*, I wish to comment on a couple things regarding the foreword by Young's friend, C. Baxter Kruger. It is clear that he is also committed to UR.[17] Over several pages he asserts that every human being is in Christ, in his death and resurrection; therefore, all are saved and no one is lost or unsaved (4-5, 9-11). Yet Kruger never makes the distinction found in the contexts of the passages he cites, such as 2 Corinthians 5 and Ephesians 2, that those who are in Christ are those who have believed and have exercised faith in Christ, but the rest who do not exercise faith are separated from him, come under the judgment of God, and will be lost everlastingly.

Kruger is also wrong to assert that Paul Young stands "in the mainstream of historic Christian confession about Jesus's identity" in his union with all humanity (10, 12). He and Paul Young assert that they are orthodox because they adhere to the Nicene Creed, yet church history affirms just the opposite. The church identified universalism as heresy in the sixth century (see my treatment of church history and universalism in my forthcoming book on universalism). Only universalists interpret the Bible to affirm, wrongly, that all, saved and unsaved, are alike united in Christ. Appendices 1 to 3 illustrate how the Nicene Creed and Athanasius differ from what Kruger and Young affirm. Kruger and Young are not orthodox.

---

17   See Baxter's website: *Perichoresis, www.perichoresis.org/.*

Young's Own Insincere Disclaimers

Another thing that concerns me is Young's own introduction. In several ways, Young tries to say that his list of lies is not to be considered "final or absolute" or "complete" (18, 20). He offers his essays as "exploring interconnected concepts" and "ideas and questions to ponder" (20, 21), yet he "proposes" these ideas as "truth" and claims that he once believed what he now labels "lies" (20). He also praises Kruger for the foreword, but the previous section indicates that Kruger is a confirmed universalist, and the "interconnected concepts" are all bound around the idea of universal reconciliation.

But more needs to be said. How long can Young keep writing as a universalist and still pass it off as "questions to ponder," as though he has not made up his mind? This presentation seems disingenuous.

Note how long Young has been a self-confessed universalist. He wholeheartedly embraced UR in 2004 in writing, and probably converted to it a year or more before. Then, sometime between 2006 and 2007, he went out of his way in a church foyer to tell my wife and me that he followed universal reconciliation, not general universalism. Then he wrote the first edition of *The Shack* for his kids, and it was full of UR (as he and his editors admitted online). After that, he wrote three novels with clear universalist attacks on evangelical faith, which correspond to those in his *Lies* book. Now he writes the book about the "lies." Finally, note that it is characteristic of universalists to protest being pinned down. In the 1920s, a universalist, when asked where universalists stand, said, "We don't stand at all. We move."[18]

For over thirteen years, Paul Young has been writing in defense of UR and weaving it into his novels. He has never publicly disavowed it during this time. Anyone can conclude from this history that he is insincere when he says that these "lies" are proposals, especially since in thirteen years he has never presented the case for traditional Christian beliefs alongside his new beliefs, except in a negative light. He seems to be bent on a crusade to change evangelical faith.

Recall from above what Young asserted about his own sense of where he stands in history (in his interview with *Religious News Service*). He

---

18   Ernest Cassara, *Universalism in America* (Boston: Beacon Press, 1971), 44.

said that the evangelical church is crumbling and that he stands on the cusp of a new reformation which the Holy Spirit is leading![19]

Whose Lies Are They?

How else can one interpret his use of *lies* in the title of his book that takes on twenty-eight Christian beliefs? If he were still searching for truth, he could have used words like *proposals* or *questions* in the title of his book. Rather, he speaks as one quite convinced of his beliefs. His use of the word *lies* is not limited to the title of his book and to each of the twenty-eight chapters. The word occurs in many more places throughout these chapters and in his novel *Cross Roads*. Young is quite deliberate in using the word.

Young arrogantly writes as one who would tell Christians that for two thousand years they have been believing the wrong things that are contrary to what he defines as "truth." He would correct and rewrite Christian history and theology.

One other matter concerns what I related above: Young came to my home in 2007 and said he was no longer a believer in UR. The book *Lies* shows that he was not telling the truth. Why does this matter? Because Paul Young presents himself as a Christian (note the full title, *Lies We Believe about God*), when he does not seem to be. He publicly confesses his many moral sins, but never his doctrinal sins. His supposed "openness" in public meetings appears to be a self-serving attempt to lead people to buy into his brand of an adulterated Christianity without giving a fair warning from where he is coming.

By emotional manipulation he gains the sympathy of his audiences for his personal struggles and thus for his books. Then he engages in sentimental self-indulgence in the plots of his novels.

The subtitle of my book *Burning Down the Shack* reads *How the "Christian" Bestseller Is Deceiving Millions*. These words were true in 2010. They are now validated. Once again, perhaps millions more will

---

19 Recently, in a blog on his website (wmpaulyoung.com/i-want-to-be-more-like-oprah-watch-interview) dated July 16, 2017, in an article titled, "Does 'The Shack' Teach Universalism?" Young declared: "We are in a time of intense transition in the landscape of Western theology." In his interview with Oprah Winfrey (dated July 9, 2017), he said that we are living in a transition time where relationship is supreme and it is the answer to all our conflicts.

buy another book that clearly is intended to lead people away from the truth of the Bible.

But one more thing must be said about his introduction. Young appeals to the Holy Spirit as "your true teacher" and says God will lead readers into the truth (20). In light of the content of his book, which is heresy, it is more correct to say something else. His book will deceive Christians regarding the content of the Bible and turn them away by Satanic deception from the truth that is in Christ Jesus (John 14:6). If Paul Young was seeking what the Holy Spirit teaches, he would follow what the Holy Spirit has already taught – the way of salvation and the eternal destinies of the lost and saved. Note the warning of 1 John 2:24-27 about remaining in the apostolic truth:

> See that what you have heard from the beginning remains in you. If it does, you also will remain in the Son and in the Father. And this is what he promised us – even eternal life. I am writing these things to you about those who are trying to lead you astray. As for you, the anointing you received from him remains in you, and you do not need anyone to teach you. But as his anointing teaches you about all things and as that anointing is real, not counterfeit – just as it has taught you, remain in him.

Concerns about the Title

Finally, I wish to draw attention to the title of Paul Young's book. It incorporates several significant terms. The first is *lies*. In his novel *Cross Roads*, chapter 13, Young attacks evangelical beliefs as "lies" eight different times. So Paul is not averse to using such a strong word. One would think that if his book is only an exploration, he could have said something like "explorations in seeking the truth about God" or some other terminology.

The word *we* is interesting. Who does *we* represent? Apparently, Paul intends it to stand for Christians or evangelicals who believe in God and that he means to speak with and for them. But as I've already pointed out and as the following pages will clarify, these aren't lies that Christians believe. Why didn't Paul use *I* or *Christians*? Again, it seems that there is deception in Young's use of this word, and he does not count himself as among Christians as they understand the term – as he clarifies in his book (55-57). Note also that the Jesus of his novel disavows the desire to make anyone a Christian (*The Shack*, 181-182).

Indeed, the book should have been titled, *Lies Paul Young Believes About God*, because the book is all about him – in both the doctrines he attacks and the stories he tells. But then the whole content of the book would have had to be reversed. The review that follows will bear out whether or not these are Paul's lies.

The Procedure

In the following pages, I review all twenty-eight chapters/lies, chapter by chapter. In each case I identify whether the "lie" is a lie, a half-truth, a full truth, or a fabricated straw man. A straw man, according to the dictionary, is a weak argument set up by an opponent so he can demolish it and gain an easy, showy victory. Many of these twenty-eight statements are straw men. The real or actual truth is far more complex and difficult to destroy. Another term for this kind of statement is a *red herring*. The dictionary defines this as "something used to divert attention from the basic issue," which describes many of the statements in *Lies*. Indeed, the many stories in these chapters raise sympathy for Paul Young's theology. It is emotional manipulation again.

Because many of the twenty-eight chapters of *Lies* overlap with the content of other chapters and deal with the same large topic, I've rearranged the chapters under four broad headings/topics of beliefs or doctrines. By this rearrangement, I believe that my exposure of Young's book is more helpful and useable than the somewhat random nature of the topics discussed by Young. This arrangement allows the readers to read all the material on a given topic in one place. It also allows me to avoid needless repetition that would be necessary in covering similar chapters.

The naming of the categories and the decision as to which chapters go into them is my work alone. It may not seem apparent at first why I brought certain chapters together, but I think subsequent treatment will make this clear.

In each part, I identify the topic or doctrine. Then I list several questions that deal with the doctrine. Finally, I list the chapters from *Lies* that I discuss under each part.

In each chapter, I first summarize the case that Young makes for calling a particular Christian belief a "lie." Then I give what I call the "Biblical Response" to each "lie." From time to time, I make reference to Young's three novels where similar material is found.

PART ONE

ANTHROPOLOGY: THE STUDY OF HUMANITY

Questions

Does God love us? What is the nature of human beings? Who is a Christian? Is God a Christian? Is Paul Young a Christian?
Is everyone a child of God? Is anyone a sinner?

Chapter 1: "God loves us, but doesn't like us."

Chapter 5: "God is a Christian."

Chapter 12: "God created (my) religion."

Chapter 14: "God doesn't care about what I'm passionate about."

*Chapter 24: "Not everyone is a child of God."

In this first section, I review those chapters that deal with human beings and their standing before God and with God. In most Christian theologies, separate sections deal with humanity in general and its condition (anthropology), sin (hamartiology), and then with Christians and how people are saved (soteriology). But because of his universal reconciliation (UR), Young treats these doctrines together and intermixes them. He says all people already are God's children and no one is lost. There is no such thing as total or even partial depravity. But for sake of greater clarity, I will deal with salvation – how people come to be God's children – in the last part of this book. The asterisk reveals what I believe to be the most important chapter in this part.

CHAPTER 1

"GOD LOVES US, BUT DOESN'T LIKE US"

(*Lies*, chapter 1)

Summary

God loves every person the same, and all are of special worth to God.

In this chapter, Young deals with the Christian "lie" that "God loves us, but doesn't like us." He seeks to show that the statement "God loves you" is not powerful or persuasive enough. Thus, he tells people that "God is especially fond of you," that God both loves and likes every human being. Young asserts that this statement can and should be made of every human being, because every person is of worth to God. It parallels similar statements in *The Shack* that God loves all his children the same and equally (*The Shack,* 154-163). Thus, we come to one of the basic assertions of universal reconciliation: every human being is a child of God.

The Biblical Response

While this discussion may help us think about a difference between loving and liking or being fond of someone, I don't believe that such terminology pertains to God and his love. Scripture affirms that "God loves the world" (John 3:16); and when God "loves," his love is full and absolute without shades of dislike. God is love and God loves (1 John 4:8). The first part describes God's nature, the second his actions. Both are totally pure and compatible. This means that God both loves and likes the objects of this kind of love. Christians have always affirmed this. While people may distinguish between loving and liking, it seems that there is no biblical basis for saying that God both loves and likes (or dislikes). All those whom God loves, he always also likes. So here Young's statement is a straw-man argument.

However, this is not the real issue that Young is attempting to confront. As one who embraces UR, his whole discussion flows out of the lack of distinction about the various ideas or definitions of love that the Bible asserts. His assertions in *The Shack* are that God loves all of his children the same and that all people are God's children. While the first part, that God loves all of his children, is true, the second is not. It is not true and is unbiblical to assert that all people are God's children.

I discuss this concept further when I respond to Paul Young's attempt to argue that everyone is a child of God from his chapter 24 in *Lies*. See my more complete discussion in chapter 5.

Differing Kinds of Love and Children of God

The Bible describes differing kinds of love and differing kinds of God's children. It distinguishes those who are God's children and those who are not, those who have repented and embraced Christ as their Savior and Lord and those who have not:

> He came to that which was his own, but his own did not receive him. Yet to all who received him, to those who believed in his name, he gave the right to become children of God – children born not of natural descent, nor of human decision or a husband's will, but born of God. (John 1:11-13)

> For in him we live and move and have our being. As some of your own poets have said, "We are his offspring." Therefore since we are God's offspring, we should not think that the divine being is like gold or silver or stone – an image made by man's design and skill. In the past God overlooked such ignorance, but now he commands all people everywhere to repent. (Acts 17:28-30)

The Apostle Paul is saying that all people are the "offspring" (note the word "offspring"; Paul does not use the word "children") of God by virtue of the fact that God has created them. God did create all people, but these same ones need to repent and believe in Christ as Savior to become his children. Acts 17:30 distinguishes the latter, the believers, from the offspring of God in Acts 17:28-29. Faith is necessary to be born again and become true children of God. It is the difference between being physically born and being born again or spiritually born – to be born from above, as Jesus makes clear in John 3.

Thus God has a general providential love for all people, as John 3:16 indicates: *God so loved the world that he gave his one and only Son*. But this is not the deeper, familial love that he has for the children born again into his family. Note 1 John 2:29-3:2:

> *If you know that he is righteous, you know that everyone*
> *who does what is right has been born of him. How great is*
> *the love the Father has lavished on us, that we should be*
> *called children of God! And this is what we are! The reason*
> *the world does not know us is that it did not know him. Dear*
> *friends, now we are children of God, and what we will be*
> *has not yet been made known. But we know that when he*
> *appears, we shall be like him, for we shall see him as he is.*

This text and many others distinguish the children of God from those who are not, whom John calls *the world*. John also emphasizes the new birth elsewhere (note 1 John 3:9-10; 5:1-5), as does the Apostle Peter:

> *In his great mercy he has given us new birth into a living hope*
> *through the resurrection of Jesus Christ from the dead. . . .*
> *As obedient children, do not conform to the evil desires you*
> *had when you lived in ignorance. . . . For you have been born*
> *again, not of perishable seed, but of imperishable, through the*
> *living and enduring word of God.* (1 Peter 1:3, 14, 23)

Also, corresponding to the idea that there are different kinds of God's children, there are different kinds of love – perhaps as many as five that fit into the one English and Greek word for "love." These ideas come from D. A. Carson; see my *Burning Down the Shack*, chapter 11. These are:

1. God's intra-trinitarian love among the Persons of the Godhead.

   The Father loves the Son and has placed everything in his hands. (John 3:35)

   For the Father loves the Son and shows him all he does. Yes, to your amazement he will show him even greater things than these. (John 5:20)

   But the world must learn that I love the Father and that I do exactly what my Father has commanded me. (John 14:31)

2. His providential love.

   This kind of love refers to God's benevolence or kindness that he shows to all humanity in his capacity as creator and sustainer of all things. The life we live, the breath we breathe, and every good thing are gifts from God, the Apostle Paul says (Acts 17:25). In the Sermon on the Mount, Jesus gives the clearest expression to this kind of love. He says:

   But I tell you: Love your enemies and pray for those who persecute you, that you may be sons of your Father in heaven. He causes his sun to rise on the evil and the good, and sends rain on the righteous and unrighteous. (Matthew 5:44-45)

   Jesus lays down a general principle regarding this providential love. He reminds his listeners that they should not worry about their lives, what they will eat or drink, or what they will wear. God will provide for these basic necessities, just as he provides food for the birds and enables the flowers and grass of the field to grow. Whatever sunshine, rain, and food that people have comes from God. Jesus exhorts his hearers to seek first the kingdom of God, and then all these other things will be given to them as well (Matthew 6:25-34).

3. His saving love for the world, conditioned on faith.

   For God so loved the world that he gave his one and only Son,

*that whoever believes in him shall not perish but have eternal
life.* (John 3:16)

4. His special, effective love for the elect, which can never fail.

   *The LORD did not set his affection on you and choose you
   because you were more numerous than other peoples, for you
   were the fewest of all peoples. But it was because the LORD
   loved you and kept the oath he swore to your forefathers that
   he brought you out with a mighty hand and redeemed you
   from the land of slavery, from the power of Pharaoh king of
   Egypt.* (Deuteronomy 7:7-8)

   *And we know that in all things God works for the good of
   those who love him, who have been called according to his
   purpose. For those God foreknew he also predestined to be
   conformed to the likeness of his Son, that he might be the first-
   born among many brothers and sisters. And those he predestined, he also called; those he called, he also justified; those he
   justified, he also glorified.* (Romans 8:28-30)

   *Husbands, love your wives, just as Christ loved the church and
   gave himself up for her.* (Ephesians 5:25)

5. His love for his own, conditioned on their obedience.

   *But showing love to a thousand generations of those who love
   me and keep my commandments.* (Exodus 20:6)

   *Now, LORD, the God of Israel, keep for your servant David my
   father the promises you made to him when you said, "You shall
   never fail to have a man to sit before me on the throne of Israel,
   if only your sons are careful in all they do to walk before me
   according to my law, as you have done."* (2 Chronicles 6:16)

   *The LORD is compassionate and gracious, slow to anger,
   abounding in love. He will not always accuse, nor will he
   harbor his anger forever; he does not treat us as our sins*

deserve or repay us according to our iniquities. For as high as
the heavens are above the earth, so great is his love for those
who fear him; as far as the east is from the west, so far has he
removed our transgressions from us.

As a father has compassion on his children, so the LORD
has compassion on those who fear him; for he knows how we
are formed, he remembers that we are dust. As for man, his
days are like grass, he flourishes like a flower of the field; the
wind blows over it and it is gone, and its place remembers it
no more. But from everlasting to everlasting the LORD's love
is with those who fear him, and his righteousness with their
children's children – with those who keep his covenant and
remember to obey his precepts. (Psalm 103:8-18)

As the Father has loved me, so have I loved you. Now remain
in my love. If you keep my commands, you will remain in my
love, just as I have obeyed my Father's commands and remain
in his love. (John 15:9-10)

Please note that it is important that these "loves" should not be treated
in isolation from each other, but should be integrated and balanced.
Note also that some love is unconditional, but the last love listed above
is not. To say that God loves everyone the same is true of the second,
providential love, but not of the third or fourth.

Let no one question the depth of love that God the Father had for
all humanity when he gave his special, unique Son to become the sin
offering for all of us (John 3:16). The world has never known such love
as that of the Father.

Let no one wonder about the depth of the love of Jesus Christ, who
became my substitute – took my place – on the cross and bore the weight
of the eternal punishment that my sin and my guilt deserved (Romans
6:23). He who had never known sin in any shape or form became fully
identified with sin for us, in our place, so we might become the perfection of God's righteousness received from Christ. Second Corinthians
5:21 affirms this: *God made him who had no sin to be sin for us, so that*
in him we might become the righteousness of God. And Jesus did this

when I was his enemy, hating him and going my own way (Romans 5:1-11). No greater love than this will ever be exercised for all eternity and in all the universe.

This discussion of the biblical distinctions regarding both the children of God and the love of God clarifies much of what Paul Young is trying to do. His failure to make such distinctions arises not from the Bible, but from his presuppositions based in universalism. Because of its basic beliefs, UR cannot afford to make such distinctions. And for UR to distinguish the love of the God of the Old Testament from that of Jesus of the New Testament is a false dichotomy.

Humanity as the Image of God

Finally, in this chapter Young has his story character ask whether there is anything in her that is "worth loving" (27). The biblical answer is yes. All humanity stands at the apex of God's creative work, which God described as *very good* (Genesis 1). All people are made in the image and likeness of God; therefore, they bear the divine image. So all are of tremendous worth. But all humanity fell into sin when Adam sinned. The image of God in all humanity has been tainted and corrupted so much that people are no longer in relationship with God as his special children. *Therefore, just as sin entered the world through one man, and death through sin, and in this way death came to all men, because all sinned – for before the law was given, sin was in the world* (Romans 5:12-13).

But people still bear the image made in God's likeness. Even though in Adam all have rebelled against God, God has provided a way back into his blessings and relationship via the cross of Christ. *For if, by the trespass of the one man, death reigned through that one man, how much more will those who receive God's abundant provision of grace and of the gift of righteousness reign in life through the one man, Jesus Christ. Consequently, just as the result of one trespass was condemnation for all men, so also the result of one act of righteousness was justification that brings life for all men* (Romans 5:17-18). For Young, as a true universalist, to fail to explain how his story character – or anyone – can find her way back to a loving God by faith is the greatest sin of omission in the history of the world. That is why UR is so evil.

Much of what I've discussed above regarding Young's first chapter ("God loves us, but doesn't like us") shows that this "lie" is mostly a straw-man type of argument. This discussion spills over to the "lie" of his twenty-fourth chapter, "Not everyone is a child of God."

CHAPTER 2

"GOD IS A CHRISTIAN"

(*Lies*, chapter 5)

Summary

Young begins his chapter 5 by telling of his personal, "life-long struggle with conflicts between faith and religion" (52). The writing of *The Shack* was to deal with this struggle. He originally wrote it for his children, and then it became a best seller for adults.

Young is not giving full disclosure regarding *The Shack*. In his paper of 2004, he identified universal reconciliation (UR) as making him a new person – as transforming him. Apparently this conversion helped him in his conflicts. In chapter 13 of *Lies*, Young finally acknowledges his conversion to UR.

In addition, Young omits the fact that there was another step between the edition that he wrote for his children and the final form of his novel. He spent a year with two pastor friends, removing the universalism as best they could from the novel to make it palatable for evangelical Christians. They acknowledged this on the website of Wayne Jacobsen and Brad Cummings. The novel people have purchased is the second edition.

Young goes on to discuss criticisms that he has received for the content of his novel. Strangely, he does not mention the subtle UR in it as one of the criticisms – something several reviewers besides me have pointed out. Why this silence?

Young addresses one of the criticisms, which is the focus of this "lie." It is Young's discourse in *The Shack* that has Jesus deny that he is a Christian. (Again, he is not giving full disclosure here, for an important part of this conversation on pages 181-182 of the novel is his having Jesus say that he doesn't try to make anyone become a Christian.) Thus, Young embarks on instructing his readers that the word *Christian* was originally an insult directed at the followers of Jesus; he says it meant "little Christs" or "mini Messiahs."

Whether or not the term *Christian* was a word of derision is not clear. Research on the word shows that it was used first in Acts 11:26 to refer to the many gentile believers at Antioch who came to faith in Christ. It may have been a term of derision, or it may have been a good term, a self-designation by Christians to separate themselves as believing gentiles from believing or unbelieving Jews. The authors and editors of most commentaries and Bible dictionaries are not sure. Subsequent uses in Acts 26:28 (Agrippa not being persuaded to become a Christian) and 1 Peter 4:16 (suffering as a Christian) and by several extra-biblical sources, both Christian and non-Christian, support both views. The passive voice "were called" suggests that it was a term created by others for Christians, and again this could be a derogatory use or could have been used to mark them as separate from Jews.

But Young has another, greater reason for this whole discussion, and it concerns the making of categories, such as Christian and non-Christian. Making categories is the issue he emphasizes, and his opposition to them flows out of his universalism. In summary, to use the terms *Christian* and *non-Christian* is to create categories, which divide people, when according to UR, all people are God's children, as Young presents in other chapters. He develops his argument through several points.

1. Young dislikes categories because it means that we "humans have manufactured [them] in order to confiscate God and God's 'blessings' over to our side of the ledger" (54).

2. Jesus is the Creator and Redeemer of every single human being. There are no outsiders and insiders, as though the latter "prayed a prayer or did something special" that moved one from the outside to the inside (55).

3. So God is not a "Christian" if he treats people differently, as outsiders or insiders; but he is a Christian if we mean that God relates to all people "as beloved insiders" (55).

4. Paul Young appeals to the Greek word *kategoro* (it should be spelled *kategoreo*), "to accuse," to define it as giving us the English *categorize*. Many categories are necessary to life, but Young asserts that if we put people into categories regarding the faith, we are doing what the devil does: *For the accuser . . . accuses them before our God day and night* – he makes categories (Revelation 12:10).

5. Using categories is wrong because "believing" is "an activity, not a category" (57). Every person is on the journey between belief and unbelief, so it is wrong to use "believer" and "unbeliever" (57).

6. Paul Young responds to the question of whether or not he is a Christian. If it means "little Christ," then the answer is yes. He embraces this categorization (57).

7. He agrees with Robert Capon that Christianity is not a religion. The cross is the sign that God has gone out of the religion business (58).

The Biblical Response

To these various points I give the following responses. In almost all of Young's points he attempts to say the following: While some categories of life are necessary, the ones that divide people into believers and unbelievers are contrary to what God does and what Jesus did at the cross; they are demonic – it is what the devil does.

1. Regarding the first point, I note that humans did not manufacture this distinction regarding faith or believer, but God and Christ Jesus in the Bible did, as expressed by the apostles in a multitude of texts:

For God so loved the world that he gave his one and only

Son, that whoever believes in him shall not perish but have eternal life. For God did not send his Son into the world to condemn the world, but to save the world through him. Whoever believes in him is not condemned, but whoever does not believe stands condemned already because they have not believed in the name of God's one and only Son. (John 3:16-18)

I am not ashamed of the gospel, because it is the power of God for the salvation of everyone who believes: first for the Jew, then for the Gentile. For in the gospel the righteousness from God is revealed, a righteousness that is by faith from first to last, just as it is written: "The righteous will live by faith." (Romans 1:16-17)

He did it to demonstrate his justice at the present time, so as to be just and the one who justifies those who have faith in Jesus. (Romans 3:26)

That if you confess with your mouth, "Jesus is Lord," and believe in your heart that God raised him from the dead, you will be saved. For it is with your heart that you believe and are justified, and it is with your mouth that you confess and are saved. (Romans 10:9-10)

Know that a man is not justified by observing the law, but by faith in Jesus Christ. So we, too, have put our faith in Christ Jesus that we may be justified by faith in Christ and not by observing the law, because by observing the law no one will be justified. (Galatians 2:16)

See to it, brothers, that none of you has a sinful, unbelieving heart that turns away from the living God. . . . So we see that they were not able to enter, because of their unbelief. . . . And without faith it is impossible to please God, because anyone who comes to him must believe that he exists and that he rewards those who earnestly seek him. (Hebrews 3:12, 19; 11:6)

Along with John 1:11-13, which I have already referenced, many, many more verses speak of those who have faith as opposed to those who do not. Faith is mentioned over six hundred times in the New Testament.

2. In the second point, Young mocks the way that many Christians have become believers. But, whether they pray a prayer or not, all must believe in order to be saved – to become a Christian. As Paul told the Philippian jailor, *Believe in the Lord Jesus, and you will be saved – you and your household* (Acts 16:31).

3. The third point is Paul Young's lie, since God treats believers differently from unbelievers, giving eternal life to the former and allowing unbelievers to go to everlasting torment. *Whoever believes in the Son has eternal life, but whoever rejects the Son will not see life, for God's wrath remains on him* (John 3:36). *Then they will go away to eternal punishment, but the righteous to eternal life* (Matthew 25:46). Many other texts, including John 3:16-17, support the fact that God treats believers and unbelievers differently.

4. The fourth point is the improper use of etymology based on the Greek word. Our English may have nothing to do with the Greek meaning, which is "to accuse," and this has nothing to do with making categories.

5. Point number five is silly, since "believer" is both an activity (it can be rendered "one who believes," as a participle) and a noun in its use in both English and Greek. Plus, the Bible never treats anyone as being somewhere on the journey of faith, but speaks repeatedly of believers and unbelievers. No one is partway on the journey to heaven or hell. To become a Christian is simply to believe the gospel. It is not a question of how much faith a person has. A decision of faith determines destiny. It is wishful thinking, and unbiblical, if Young would place a person like Hitler on the journey to faith. Young confuses salvation with

sanctification, the latter word meaning that one is in a process of growing mature as a Christian.

6. & 7. It seems inconsistent that Paul Young would embrace this kind of categorization in point 6. In a sense, number 7 reflects the truth of the Bible as a unique revelation from God. The knowledge of God revealed in Jesus Christ is unique, but there is a sense, such as in an American census, in which Christians would identify themselves as belonging to the Christian religion as distinct from Islam, Hinduism, Buddhism, etc. "Christian" is also a common word that church fathers used to compare Christianity to other religions of the Roman world (see appendix 2 on Athanasius).

The overall impact of this chapter is consistent with UR and other chapters to be discussed. Another consistency with UR is evident: the source of much of what Young believes comes not from the Bible, but from his own head, from past heresies, from the devil, the deceiver, and from wishful thinking. One thing Young has apparently overlooked is what the Bible says about all these issues, including who is a Christian. It is arrogant for Young or anyone to disregard what the Lord Jesus Christ says and set himself up as an authority in place of the Bible. Such a person does not have either Christ or the Father, according to the Apostle John: *Anyone who runs ahead and does not continue in the teaching of Christ does not have God; whoever continues in the teaching has both the Father and the Son. If anyone comes to you and does not bring this teaching, do not take him into your house or welcome him. Anyone who welcomes him shares in his wicked work* (2 John 9-11).

The "lie" of this chapter is a straw man. No mature Christian would affirm that God is a Christian, since a Christian is a disciple, a follower, of Christ. Rather, the Father *sent his Son as an atoning sacrifice* [the propitiation] *for our sins* (1 John 4:10). To assert that God is a Christian is a straw man, and it is also false.

CHAPTER 3

"GOD CREATED (MY) RELIGION"

(*Lies*, chapter 12)

Summary

In chapter 12, Young takes issue with calling Christianity a religion, calling it instead a mutual relationship of people with God. He faults institutions in general.

This chapter builds on other chapters where Young goes to the heart of his universal reconciliation (UR): God is love, and every human being is already his child and in relationship with him. In other chapters, Young pursues other aspects of this foundational belief.

After citing a funny story, Young makes his point that Christianity is not a religion. He asserts this by focusing on one part of the dictionary definition of religion that deals with the institutional aspect of religion. By this part of the definition, Young determines that religion is about performance and behavior. Christianity is not a religion by this definition, because Christianity is about a relationship with God and others, and to this relationship, God "submits." Note the "lie" of *Lies*, chapter 4: "God does not submit."

Young continues to fault Christianity as an institution because it "almost always" embodies both destructive and beneficial elements – destructive because it becomes a means to control others. Young appeals to the derivation of *religion* from the Latin *religio,* which he says means "to bind oneself back to God." This meaning suggests that religion will develop into performance and away from relationship. Instead, Jesus "is in us" and invites us to look to him for everything, so that there is no division between the sacred and secular, to participate in the life of God.

Continuing on this theme, Young faults institutions because people "routinely become controlled by the very systems and institutions they create" (113). He closes this chapter by praising the Old Testament institutions of the Sabbatical Year and the Year of Jubilee, when all the land was given rest and debts and liabilities were forgiven.

The Biblical Response

Young is a bit less extreme in his denunciation of institutions in chapter 12 than in some statements he makes in *The Shack* novel (they're missing in the film). His evaluation of Christianity as not being a religious institution is only a half truth. While our relationship with God through knowing Jesus Christ is of greatest importance, Christianity does have an institutional side (2 John 9-11). The church is primarily people, but the institutional aspect is represented by the fact that believers gather at least once a week and follow the pattern laid down in the New Testament. The earliest believers met in some place, and they were instructed by pastors, elders, and deacons in the faith and learned to serve one another:

> To the elders among you, I appeal as a fellow elder and a witness of Christ's sufferings and one who also will share in the glory to be revealed: Be shepherds of God's flock that is under your care, serving as overseers – not because you must, but because you are willing, as God wants you to be; not greedy for money, but eager to serve; not lording it over those entrusted to you, but being examples to the flock. And when the Chief Shepherd appears, you will receive the crown of glory that will never fade away. (1 Peter 5:1-4)

> If anyone sets his heart on being an overseer, he desires a noble task. Now the overseer must be above reproach, the husband of but one wife, temperate, self-controlled, respectable, hospitable, able to teach. . . . He must not be a recent convert, or he may become conceited and fall. . . . Deacons, likewise, are

*to be men worthy of respect. . . . They must keep hold of the
deep truths of the faith with a clear conscience. They must
first be tested; and then if there is nothing against them, let
them serve as deacons. . . . If I am delayed, you will know how
people ought to conduct themselves in God's household, which
is the church of the living God, the pillar and foundation of the
truth.* (1 Timothy 3:1-15)

*They devoted themselves to the apostles' teaching and to fel-
lowship, to the breaking of bread and to prayer.* (Acts 2:42)

Early Christians embraced creeds, as seen in Colossians 1:15-20 and
Philippians 2:6-11, and they met to worship, as evidenced in Acts 2:1,
14:1, 16:13, and 1 Corinthians 16:1-2. They gave money and resources,
participated in collections for others, and did other things together.
Paramount for believers was the regular observance of communion
(the Lord's Supper) and the baptizing of new believers.

In all of Young's writings, I have read virtually nothing about the
need to observe these two ordinances of the church. Yet on the night
of his betrayal, Jesus commanded the observance of communion, as
pointing to his death:

*While they were eating, Jesus took bread, gave thanks, and
broke it, and gave it to his disciples, saying, "Take and eat; this
is my body."*

*Then he took the cup, gave thanks, and offered it to them, say-
ing, "Drink from it, all of you. This is my blood of the covenant, which is poured out for many for the forgiveness of sins.
I tell you, I will not drink of this fruit of the vine from now on
until that day when I drink it anew with you in my Father's
kingdom.* (Matthew 26:26-29)

Paul the Apostle exhorts his readers to observe communion, because
in doing so they are doing what the Lord said and they are doing it in
remembrance of Jesus:

*For I received from the Lord what I also passed on to you:
The Lord Jesus, on the night he was betrayed, took bread, and*

*when he had given thanks, he broke it and said, "This is my
body, which is for you; do this in remembrance of me." In the
same way, after supper he took the cup, saying, "This cup is
the new covenant in my blood; do this, whenever you drink
it, in remembrance of me. "For whenever you eat this bread
and drink this cup, you proclaim the Lord's death until he
comes. Therefore, whoever eats the bread or drinks the cup
of the Lord in an unworthy manner will be guilty of sinning
against the body and blood of the Lord. A man ought to examine himself before he eats of the bread and drinks of the cup.*
(1 Corinthians 11:23-28)

Also, in the Great Commission, Jesus claimed that all authority in
heaven and earth was given to him. He then commanded his followers to make disciples of all nations, to baptize them in the name of the
Triune God, and to teach them *to obey everything I have commanded
you* (Matthew 28:19-20).

I have wondered why Young makes no mention of these ordinances.
It probably has something to do with his aversion to any thought of
obedience, authority, or submission. But note that to fail to observe these
ordinances means failure to *remember his death* and failure to make
disciples! What is more, it is called the "communion" service; it is one
of the chief means of developing and growing a person's relationship
with God. Relationship is probably the biggest point in Young's UR, yet
he says nothing about this biblical pattern for developing relationship.

By this failure, Young rejects the memory of Jesus and the meaning of Christ's death. He disobeys him and thus cannot claim to have a
relationship with him and with God. His failure to encourage the Lord's
Supper is by itself enough reason to reject Young's whole structure based
in UR. Peter warned us of those like Young who are false teachers, who
*secretly introduce destructive heresies, even denying the sovereign Lord
who bought them – bringing swift destruction on themselves* (2 Peter 2:1).
He is destined for the *blackest darkness*, as described in verses 12-13 in
the book of Jude: *These men are blemishes at your love feasts, eating with
you without the slightest qualm – shepherds who feed only themselves.
They are clouds without rain, blown along by the wind; autumn trees,*

without fruit and uprooted – twice dead. They are wild waves of the sea, foaming up their shame; wandering stars, for whom blackest darkness has been reserved forever.

In addition, as I pointed out earlier, Christianity is a religion when we compare it with other religions, such as Islam, Hinduism, or Buddhism. Church fathers such as Athanasius used the term *Christianity* when comparing it to the religions of the Roman world (see appendix 2 on Athanasius).

Regarding relationship, Young characteristically places relationship in opposition to performance and doing something, but the two go together. Jesus himself said that if we love him, we will obey him (John 14-16). Our doing, our works, prove that we have genuine faith and love. Note a few statements from 1 John where this is stated emphatically:

> *Whoever claims to live in him* [have a relationship with him] *must walk as Jesus did.* (1 John 2:6)

> *The man who does the will of God lives forever.* (1 John 2:17)

> *If you know that he is righteous, you know that everyone who does what is right has been born of him.* (1 John 2:29)

And James gives us the well-known truth: *Faith without works is dead* (James 2:26 NASB). These are the concluding words of an entire chapter devoted to this principle.

Behind Young's discussion of this "lie" is what he says in his novel. In *The Shack,* Young espoused a "pure relationship," a "circle of relationship," in which there is no submission of either party and no authority exercised either by God or by people (*The Shack,* 122-124). I devoted an entire chapter of my book *Burning Down the Shack* to the fallacy of this idea and its blasphemous overtones.[20] A "pure relationship" is impossible, as even sociologists have warned. It breeds the idea of everyone doing what is right in his own eyes, and it collapses. A "circle of relationship" in which people and God are equals is impossible, because it magnifies the immanence (indwelling) of God while denying to God the glory of his supreme or surpassing transcendence that is his alone.

---

20   James De Young, *Burning Down the Shack* (Washington, D.C.: WorldNetDaily, 2010), Chapter 5: "Relationship and Obedience."

Finally, Young's words about institutions need to be opposed. He states in *The Shack* that the institutions of marriage, government, and the church are "the man-created trinity of terrors that ravages the earth and deceives those I care about" (*The Shack*, 179). He also said, "Every human institution is the matrix, a diabolical scheme" (*The Shack*, 122-124). He has God say, "I don't create institutions – never have, never will" (*The Shack*, 179). While here in *Lies*, chapter 12, Young's words are toned down a bit, he still refers to these institutions as created by people (113).

Yet God created the three institutions that Young rejects: the church (Matthew 16), the government (Romans 13:1-7), and marriage (Genesis 2; Ephesians 5). Why would Young take such a position in direct conflict with the Bible? Because his adoption of UR makes God's love supreme above all else, and this love must prevail among God's children in a relationship with him – not in some ordered or authoritative structure. Young's belief in UR overrides what the Bible says. Thus, any appeal he makes to the Bible, such as to the Bible's Year of Jubilee and Sabbatical Year, is disingenuous and hypocritical.

The "lie" of this chapter is largely a straw man.

CHAPTER 4

"GOD DOESN'T CARE WHAT I'M PASSIONATE ABOUT"

(*Lies*, chapter 14)

Summary

In chapter 14, Young takes on the passions that people pursue, and he claims that they all originate in the Triune God. Does he also guard a hidden agenda flowing from his universal reconciliation (UR)? The answer is yes.

Young begins the chapter by admitting that he has had no hobbies, except that he recently discovered the hobby of listening to others tell about their hobbies, and he enters into their passion and joy. He illustrates this by telling the story of his friend who also embraces UR. This friend is the C. Baxter Kruger who wrote the foreword to *Lies* in which he advocates the reading of Young's book. Kruger found joy in being able to challenge a botanist who was a fellow passenger on a flight to the Northwest. He was able to awaken a new thought in this man by asking where his passion for discovering and classifying new plants comes from. Kruger told the man that this passion comes from the Triune God – that they were "sharing their heart and love for the creation." The scientist was "participating in the work of God" (128).

Young goes on to assert that a whole host of our desires – loving, exploring, serving, working, creating, drawing, sowing, dancing, grieving, crying, singing, fishing, or golfing – "all these desires are expressions of the very nature of a God who celebrates our life and our humanity" (129). And to get to the point of the title of his book, Young adds, "God . . . is not content to let us stay inside brokenness or the lies we have believed" (129). He goes on: "Your joy and your love . . . and your curiosity and your drive toward authenticity and integrity and your wonder all originate in God. What an amazing thought!" (129).

The Biblical Response

At first I thought, "Who can find any fault in this chapter?" But as I reflected on what Young is saying and whether his UR has any part in this, I realized that even here Young is propagating UR in subtle but consistent ways.

(1) Note the universalism of the kinds of things Young enumerates. (I've recorded only some of them.) Yet Young omits all kinds of evil passions that people may engage in, such as lying, cheating, thievery, sexual immorality of all sorts (homosexuality, lesbianism, pederasty, or prostitution, for example), and gambling, etc. Paul the Apostle gives a whole list of thirty-two vices in Romans 1, and this is only partial. So Young is thinking only of positive passions. But who decides what is positive? What makes many passions wrong or sinful? Is God then the originator of these evil passions, or do they come from within our fallen nature, as Christians have always asserted? James tells us that evil desires and the resulting behavior come from within us:

> When tempted, no one should say, "God is tempting me." For God cannot be tempted by evil, nor does he tempt anyone; but each one is tempted when, by his own evil desire, he is dragged away and enticed. Then, after desire has conceived, it gives birth to sin; and sin, when it is full-grown, gives birth to death. Don't be deceived, my dear brothers. (James 1:13-16)

Further, in Romans 6 the Apostle Paul tells us that Christians are to put off or to put to death all kinds of evil deeds and pursuits. He continues the same admonition in his letter to the Colossians:

> Put to death, therefore, whatever belongs to your earthly nature: sexual immorality, impurity, lust, evil desires, and

greed, which is idolatry. Because of these, the wrath of God is coming. You used to walk in these ways, in the life you once lived. But now you must also rid yourselves of all such things as these: Anger, rage, malice, slander, and filthy language from your lips. Do not lie to each other, since you have taken off your old self with its practices. (Colossians 3:5-9)

Isn't the Bible, what it commands, and what is in agreement with the character and nature of God as revealed in the Bible and in the creation, the touchstone or standard for what is good? This is what the Apostle Paul says in Romans:

The wrath of God is being revealed from heaven against all the godlessness and wickedness of men who suppress the truth by their wickedness, since what may be known about God is plain to them, because God has made it plain to them. For since the creation of the world God's invisible qualities – his eternal power and divine nature – have been clearly seen, being understood from what has been made, so that men are without excuse. (Romans 1:18-20)

The character of God is declared to be not only love and good and life (which Young confesses) but also holy, just, and righteous (as Romans 2 declares). I discuss this matter of character more fully in chapter 26, which covers chapter 15 of *Lies*. So Young's thinking flows from his basic understanding that humanity is "fundamentally good" (34-35), that all people are equally and fully children of God (*Lies*, chapter 24), and that God does not judge (again, see my discussion in my chapter 26). Young avoids using the word *sin* because this word suggests that people are not fundamentally good and that there is violation of the divine nature of God, which nature Young places within people, because they are in God.

(2) In support of the universalism engaged here, note that Young would have Kruger say to a person who may or may not know God that he is "participating" in God's work. Now, even evangelicals might say this in a general way – people seeking to preserve and understand the

environment all around us are sometimes working with and for God, and yet the people do not personally know God through Jesus Christ. But the context of this chapter has two followers of UR saying these words. Kruger and Young actually believe that such people really are God's children and that God is truly sharing his heart with them in the relationship that God has with all people. Because of their UR perspective, they assume a meaning for these words that is much more specific, certain, and deliberate. But from a biblical perspective, this meaning is not true. See my discussion in my chapters that take up *Lies* chapters 1, 12, and 24.

(3) Note Young's thoughts that such passions are the "very nature of a God who celebrates our life and our humanity" (129). In light of what he says elsewhere (*Lies*, chapter 10), that all humanity bears the nature of God, this statement suggests that there is divinity within all people that gives expression to these passions. This is false; human beings, even Christians, are not little deities.

(4) There is further evidence that UR is involved in the foundation of *Lies*, chapter 14. Young speaks about God's not letting people stay in the "lies we have believed" (129). This is Young's direct reference to his present book, *Lies We Believe about God*. He is determined to associate his "lies" with his purpose of changing people and their beliefs. By using terms such as "your curiosity" and "drive toward authenticity and integrity . . . all originate in God," Young is saying that the ideas and doctrines of UR are the only true ones that agree with this terminology and come from God. Implicitly he is praising curiosity and uncertainty, as he does elsewhere. He is also saying that what ideas or beliefs do not agree with those of UR are not from God and are not authentic and true. The net effect of what I've observed above is that Young cannot avoid thinking and writing about anything apart from UR. He is passionate about UR. He is very deliberate in what he writes and subversive toward Christian or biblical truth. He needs to be read very carefully and critically. He also seems to be extremely arrogant in his apparent belief that UR, and not the Bible, is truth.

I have already cited quite a list of evil behaviors. Some who practice these evil behaviors are those who practice deceit, those who are *slanderers, God-haters, insolent, arrogant and boastful* (Romans 1:29-30). These words are appropriate for those who believe in UR.

The "lie" of chapter 14 – that God doesn't care about what I'm passionate about – is a half-truth. Scripture is clear that God's will and his plans for our life are what matter, not our own passions and pursuits. Unless God is the one who puts the passion in us for something, that thing matters little to him. Young is passionate about UR, and this passion makes it necessary for Christians to qualify the opposite of this "lie."

As one thinks about the "lie" of this chapter, it becomes clear that Young uses these words to vindicate his pursuit of his own lies. He is involved in self-indulgence and wants to believe that his passion for UR originates in God.

God does care about Young's passion for UR, but not in the way Young thinks. God loves the truth but hates deceit, and we've discovered enough deceit in UR to be able to say that God hates it. Universal reconciliation slanders God and his Word, the truth.

*CHAPTER 5

"NOT EVERYONE IS A CHILD OF GOD"

(*Lies*, chapter 24)

Summary

Paul Young asserts that every human being is a child of God, whether one believes or not. He explicitly rejects the difference that some are children of God by being created by God and that others are the children of God by a second birth – a spiritual rebirth – such as Jesus taught in John 3:5 (205).

Here are the points from Young that I've identified:

1. He says that to make the distinction between those who are born again and those who are not, we declare that some are children of God and others are not. If we recognize this difference, we "rationalize" and justify the "creating of another box" to divide people into "categories," which he has already rejected on the basis of a Greek word study that I believe to be faulty (56-57). Thus, it isn't necessary that someone become a child of God, because everyone already is a child of God (205).

2. It doesn't matter what one believes or doesn't believe – even atheists are children of God (204). In his story, Young identifies an atheist acquaintance as a "good man, who loves his children, who believes in Love and Life and Truth, who is witty and kind

and generously compassionate" (208). Apparently for Young, this is sufficient to identify the person as a child of God.

3. Young cites two important texts that seemingly support no distinctions: Acts 17:28-29 (all are children of God) and Ephesians 4:5-6 (there is *one God and Father of all*) (206). But in both instances, Young betrays his special, faulty hermeneutics – how he interprets the Bible.

The Biblical Response

Here are my replies to the preceding:

(1) Jesus and the apostles make many distinctions. Chief among these are that there are believers and unbelievers, those who believe in Jesus Christ and those who don't. This whole discourse about making categories is ridiculous and false. The Bible itself makes categories when it says that God's true children are those who have received Christ and are born again, compared to those who have not received Christ and who refuse to be born again, as mentioned earlier in John 1:11-13. Note the strong categories that Jesus makes as he proclaims that those who believe have everlasting life, while those who do not are perishing. In addition to John 3:16-17, Matthew 25:46 speaks of categories with a great difference: *Then they will go away to eternal punishment, but the righteous to eternal life.*

By drawing a parallel with the children in his own family, Young seeks to illustrate how everyone is a child of God. No matter to what extent his children may seek to withdraw from their family, even changing their name, their "fundamental identity" cannot be changed. Even if they should no longer believe in their family identity, "they don't have to believe" that they are Paul's children "in order to make it true" (205).

But one must ask: Isn't Paul Young making a category when he speaks of "our children" that distinguishes them from "my children" and others? Don't his children have a different, deeper relationship with him than my children have with him? Would he treat my children exactly as he treats his? The Bible says that God's children have become co-heirs with Jesus Christ: *Now if we are children, then we are heirs – heirs of God and co-heirs with Christ* (Romans 8:17).

Does Paul Young consider my children to be equal heirs of all that his own children have as his heirs? This simple illustration shows how shallow Young's whole argument really is. In all of life, we make categories that are vital to living in harmony with others. Without such, the result is anarchy, abuse, violations, and crimes.

(2) Regarding Young's point about the requirement of faith in order to be identified as a child of God, note the strong words of John 3:18: *Whoever believes in him is not condemned, but whoever does not believe stands condemned already because he has not believed in the name of God's one and only Son.* In light of verse 16, which promises eternal life, this verse speaks of the category of perishing. In one verse, belief is mentioned three times.

In John 1:12, John writes directly about who a child of God is. *But as many as received him* [Jesus Christ], *to them he gave authority to become children of God – even to them that believe on his name.* So, whom are we to believe: Young, who denies that faith makes the difference in identifying whether one is a child of God, or Jesus, the Son of God?

Again, Young is using people's emotion to gain sympathy for his betrayal of Jesus's words.

Later in the book of John, Jesus said that he, a person, embodies *the way and the truth and the life* (John 14:6). Apparently, Young believes that someone can be a child of God and believe in the abstracts of love, life, and truth, while rejecting the Savior who alone embodies these great values as no one else in the universe ever could. Jesus's words mean that if we reject him, we cannot know or believe in the real or truest love, life, and truth. Thus, Young ends up attacking our Lord and Savior, and thereby rejects the one who truly is these most essential realities.

Further, the major point of the Bible is that it *does* matter what one believes. Faith in Jesus Christ is the one thing that a person must exercise to be saved. And while Young would dismiss this faith as a work, note that Ephesians 2:8-9 says that we are saved by means of faith, and it also denies that faith is a work that saves. Faith is our response and is always separated from works, as the Apostle Paul explains in regard to Abraham (Romans 4:1-8).

Finally, for Young to point out that his atheist friend, whom he wants to identify as a child of God, is a good man who does good things is troublesome. (a) Whether or not one is good has nothing to do with being a child of God. His identity as a child of God is solely linked to whether or not he believes. John 1:12 tells us that only those who believe have the right to be called children of God. (b) Citing his good deeds violates Ephesians 2:8-9, which says that we are saved by faith and not by works.

(3) In regard to the point about there being no distinctions in people, Young's citation of the two texts illustrates once again that he distorts the Bible by contradicting what the contexts contribute to the separate verses that he cites and he even mistranslates the words.

While Acts 17:28-29 identifies all people as God's created *offspring*, the Apostle Paul exhorts his readers that this is not enough. In the very next verses, the Apostle says that God *commands all people everywhere to repent. For he has set a day when he will judge the world with justice by the man* [Jesus Christ] *he has appointed. He has given proof of this to all men by raising him from the dead* (Acts 17:30-31). Verse 18 in that same chapter clarifies these verses by informing the reader that Paul *was preaching the good news about Jesus and the resurrection.* In light of the other preaching of Paul in Acts, it is clear that he was urging people to repent of their unbelief and to put their faith in Jesus. The last verse of the chapter says *A few men became followers of Paul and believed* (Acts 17:34).

So, while all people are descendants of God in the sense that they are his created offspring, this is not enough to know God, to be in relationship with him, or to avoid a day of judgment due to unbelief. People need to have another birth. All people have been born physically; all need to have a subsequent, spiritual new birth to enter into God's family.

I point out one more critical matter. Young misrepresents what Acts 17:28-29 says. He has misquoted the verses when he writes: "'For we also are God's children.' Being then the children of God. . . .'" The word "children" does not appear in the original Greek (which would have been a form of *teknon* or *huios*). Instead the word *genos* occurs twice. It means "family," "offspring," "race," "descendant," "kind," and so forth; but it should not be translated "child."[21] Apparently Young has chosen an unsupported translation which fits his theology but not the Greek text.

The other text, Ephesians 4:5-6, affirms that there is *one Lord, one faith, one baptism; one God and Father of all, who is over all and through all and in all.* From the context, it is clear that the Apostle Paul is describing the body of Christ – Christians. Verse 4 has *one body*; verse 12 has *the body of Christ*; verses 15-16 refer twice more to the same *body* of Christ. Clearly, then, the context of verses 5-6 points to Christians who compose the *all* mentioned four times in verse 6. Thus, *God* and *Father* each have a narrow reference here. God is the Father of Christians, not of all humanity.

Even if the terms *God* and *Father* have the general reference as they do in Acts 17:28-29, it is clear from the contexts of Acts and of Ephesians that Paul thinks only Christians are the true children of God and members of the body of Christ. Even though the Ephesians were *offspring of God* according to Acts 17, they were formerly alienated from him according to Ephesians 2. Before exercising faith in Christ, the Ephesians were dead in their *transgressions and sins* and *by nature objects of wrath* (Ephesians 2:1, 3). But they *have been saved through faith* (Ephesians 2:5, 8). Formerly they *were separate from Christ . . . without hope and without God in the world*, but *now in Christ Jesus you who once were far away have been brought near by the blood of Christ* (Ephesians 2:12-13). In Christ they now have *access to the Father by one Spirit* (Ephesians 2:18).

All these texts proclaim that the Ephesians at one point were not children of God, but because of the death of Christ, they became God's children by means of putting faith in Jesus Christ.

Just because the Apostle Paul expands on God in universal terms with the last phrase (although even here "all" may be limited to the saints), this does not mean that the Apostle is promoting universal reconciliation. It is no more than what the Apostle affirms in Acts 17.

---

21   All the standard lexicons and Bible translations (KJV, NKJV, NASV, NIV, ESV, NLB, NRSV, AB, etc.) translate the word as "offspring" here.

It is inconceivable that Paul here would contradict his emphasis in the rest of the epistle on believing. And note that he says that God's *wrath comes on those who are disobedient* (Ephesians 5:6). The present existence of God's wrath as depicted by the present-tense verb conflicts with the claims of universalism that God is not a God of wrath. Note the same present tense in Romans 1:18-19: *The wrath of God is being revealed from heaven against all the godlessness and wickedness of men, who suppress the truth by their wickedness, since what may be known about God is plain to them, because God has made it plain to them.*

The Bible is clear. Paul Young is wrong in failing to distinguish between those who are children of God in the most general sense by virtue of being created by God and those who are in the body of Christ by believing and being saved. Young is deceiving multitudes by giving them a false hope of being saved and having eternal life, when they do not have this life because they have not believed in Christ.

The "lie" of this chapter is not a lie, but is the truth. Not everyone is a child of God. Those who reject the gospel of the good news of salvation found in Jesus Christ are not the children of God. Young is the purveyor of lies.

PART TWO

THEOLOGY PROPER: THE STUDY OF GOD

Questions

Who is God? What is the nature of God? What is God like? Is God good? Is God a sexual being? Is God a prude? Is the institution of government evil? Did God torture his Son?

*Chapter 2: "God is good. I am not."

Chapter 6: "God wants to use me."

*Chapter 7: "God is more he than she."

Chapter 8: "God wants to be a priority."

Chapter 9: "God is a magician."

*Chapter 10: "God is a prude."

*Chapter 11: "God blesses my politics."

Chapter 16: "God is not good."

Chapter 20: "God is a divine Santa Claus."

Chapter 22: "God is not involved in my suffering."

Chapter 23: "You will never find God in a box."

Chapter 25: "God is disappointed in me."

Chapter 26: "God loves me for my potential."

**Chapter 28: "God is One alone."

This second section comprises many chapters. Paul Young attempts to bring clarity to the understanding of who God is – what his nature or character is. Not only do we find here some declarations typical of universal reconciliation (UR), but we find many that seem to be of Young's own creation. Indeed, some seem to border on the bizarre and perverted. For example, Young claims that people bear the divine nature of God, that they were created in God, and that God is a sexual being. Asterisks with some of the chapters above indicate their special importance, for they are especially troublesome to Christians.

*CHAPTER 6

"GOD IS GOOD. I AM NOT."

(*Lies*, chapter 2)

Summary

In his second chapter, Paul Young takes exception to the evangelical teaching that people are lost in sin prior to coming to faith and that they are either partially or totally depraved and in need of being saved.

To make the review of this chapter clearer, I've kept Young's order, but arranged his discussion into many distinctive points.

Paul Young says that this "lie" is a "huge" lie:

1. He says this "lie" means that Christians proclaim that while God is good, people are not. Christians commonly declare that God sees people as depraved and worthless and other bad things. Young provides a long litany of adjectives (30). People come to believe this, and shame accompanies such self-evaluation. Young emphasizes his own past sense of this shame by recounting that his distorted self-worth arose out of verbal denunciations given from a father who was a missionary.

2. But Young objects to this "lie" of Christians. He argues that people have "inherent value" because they are made in the "image of God" (32-33).

3. Young particularly focuses on those who preach the "gospel." He faults them for proclaiming that people are "totally depraved"

and "worthless." They preach this message: "May God have mercy on your soul!" (34).

4. Young counters that people do not have a "core of ungoodness," but are "true and right," that they are "blind, not depraved" in their condition (34-35).

5. He appeals to the fact that Christ became human to show that personhood cannot be "evil or inherently bad" (34-35).

6. Young appeals to the "essential identity" of everyone as being "fundamentally good," because all are "created in Christ," bearing God's image (35). He cites Ephesians 2:10, which says, *For we are God's workmanship, created in Christ Jesus to do good works.*

7. Young argues that God doesn't have a low view of humanity, because he created people in his image as a "very good creation" (35-36). People need to stop believing the "devastating lies" in our "deceit-darkness" (36).

The Biblical Response

This chapter is crucial because it goes to the heart of the nature of human beings and the nature of sin. Are people sinners in need of salvation because they are lost and cannot save themselves?

Young is very wrong on several of his points. All Christians believe that people are sinners in need of salvation due to the fall of Adam and Eve, when they plunged the whole world into sin and separation from God. In one view, this fall resulted in total depravity so that there is nothing in a person by which that person can take the initiative to come to God in repentance and find forgiveness (Calvinism). In the other view, the fall resulted in the collapse of humanity into sin but not total depravity, so that some good enables people to initiate their return to God to find forgiveness and be saved (Arminianism). But in either case, no Christian affirms what Paul Young does here – that people are not so bad that they need to be saved from the domination of sin. All people are already saved, as he will assert later (in *Lies*, chapter 13).

Clearly, Young objects to the Calvinist view on humanity and sin as indicated by the terms he uses and which I've just cited. But several points above are straw men, including points 1, 3, and 7. These points are at least overstated, since no biblically informed Christian would say that people are "worthless" or that God has a "low view of humanity." Rather, Christians all affirm point number 2, because people are made in the image of God.

But Young is wrong on several more points. Regarding number 4 above, Young conveniently says nothing about the fall of Adam and Eve in Genesis 3 and how that may have affected all of humanity. The race became so evil that God had to destroy all people except one family by means of the flood (Genesis 6). The destruction of Sodom and Gomorrah illustrates that one society was so evil it had to be destroyed. Genesis 13:13 confirms this: *Now the men of Sodom were wicked and were sinning greatly against the LORD.*

Genesis 18:25 also speaks of the wickedness of the people, but distinguishes between the righteous and the wicked: *Far be it from you to do such a thing – to kill the righteous with the wicked, treating the righteous and the wicked alike.* Genesis 19 then describes the actual destruction of these cities, but the saving of Lot and his family.

In the New Testament, the Apostle Paul writes that death came to all people because of Adam, when he transgressed, and because of their own sins. *Just as sin entered the world through one man, and death through sin, and in this way death came to all men, because all sinned* (Romans 5:12). Paul also writes to the Corinthians about this same concept: *For since death came through a man, the resurrection of the dead comes also through a man. For as in Adam all die, so in Christ all will be made alive* (1 Corinthians 15:21-22). By means of his sacrificial death, Christ eliminated this spiritual death for all people who put faith in him.

Young says nothing of faith, and his statements that people are basically true and right and good are unbiblical. Young cannot and does not cite any Scripture that affirms this, but the many verses in Romans 1:18-3:19 affirm that all are not good, nor do they do good. All are sinners who come short of what pleases God (Romans 3:23). More importantly, the consequence of this "coming short" is huge and eternal: it is everlasting death. *For the wages of sin is death, but the gift of God is eternal life in Christ Jesus our Lord* (Romans 6:23).

The Apostle Paul is laying the foundation for why a sinless Savior had to come to make propitiation (an atoning sacrifice, satisfaction) available for all who believe.

> *God presented him as a sacrifice of atonement, through faith in his blood. He did this to demonstrate his justice, because in his forbearance he had left the sins committed beforehand unpunished – he did it to demonstrate his justice at the present time, so as to be just and the one who justifies those who have faith in Jesus.* (Romans 3:25-26)

So all people need to be saved from the penalty and power of sin, but Young essentially asserts that no one is in need of saving – which is his "lie" discussed in his chapter 13.

Young is also wrong on point number 5. While Christ's coming in human flesh does validate the essential value of humanity, this does not mean that humanity is free of sin or that it is not evil or bad. The essential worth of humanity goes back to Genesis 1 and 2, but Young overlooks the total contamination of sin that came in Genesis 3. He conveniently (deceptively?) ignores the biblical truth that Jesus Christ was born from a virgin and conceived by the Holy Spirit specifically so that he would not enter humanity as a fallen, sinful human being. Jesus's becoming human has a special meaning, but it doesn't mean that the race of humanity is not evil. Young's omission slanders the real nature of Jesus's incarnation. In appendix 2, I show that the early church father Athanasius (fourth century) asserts all of these great truths in his work, *The Incarnation of the Word of God.*

Young applies the Scripture *for we are God's handiwork, created in Christ Jesus to do good works* to all humanity, but this does violence to the context (Ephesians 2:10). He fails to note that all humanity is not being described here, but that being created *in Christ* refers only to Christians. Verses 8 and 9 in Ephesians 2 declare that Christians are saved by faith, not by works, and Christians are those who are *created in Christ Jesus.* Thus, all are not "fundamentally good," because failure to believe in Christ means that they are not *in Christ.*

As the Apostle writes of the Ephesians, prior to coming to faith they were *dead in transgressions and sins*, were *by nature deserving of* [God's] *wrath*, and *formerly . . . were separate from Christ . . . without hope and without God in the world* (Ephesians 2:1, 3, 12). But Jesus Christ came *to reconcile* both Jews and gentiles *in one body to God through the cross* (Ephesians 2:16). Thus, prior to their coming to faith in Christ, people were spiritually dead and deserving of the wrath of God. They are not God's intimate children; they are not "fundamentally good" prior to Christ's reconciling them.

All of the preceding points show that Young is wrong and his beliefs in this area are contrary to biblical truth. These falsehoods arise from his universalism. Again, this heresy asserts that all are children of God whether they believe or not; all are not sinners, and none need to be saved from sin. All these beliefs exist because UR ignores or distorts the Bible.

A crucial observation for understanding all the chapters of *Lies* is this: Young gives far more weight to discovering his interpretation of doctrine from people's experience than from the total teaching of the Bible. Huge swaths of the Bible are ignored, such as the fall, the flood, and the atoning sacrifice, along with biblical terminology. *Sin* is hardly ever used, but in the Bible it is a predominant word. If the Bible is not the standard for truth, there will never be a standard for truth, for everyone's experience differs from that of others.

This "lie" as stated by Young in this chapter is the absolute truth, and he is wrong to deny or correct it.

In the hymn "Rock of Ages," Augustus Toplady was more biblically correct to write:

> *Nothing in my hand I bring,*
> *Simply to Thy cross I cling;*
> *Naked, come to Thee for dress;*
> *Helpless, look to Thee for grace;*
> *Foul, I to the fountain fly;*
> *Wash me, Savior, or I die!*

CHAPTER 7

"GOD WANTS TO USE ME"

(*Lies*, chapter 6)

Summary

In chapter 6 of *Lies*, Young deals with the nature of God as one who does not use human beings as "tools," but as a God who is in relationship with all his children.

He addresses the nature or character of God by emphasizing the power of words and how they are windows into the souls of people. Words can build up or destroy. Young's point is that when people say such things as "God wants to use me," they are communicating what they think of the nature of God. These words are "more about a utilitarian god than the God of relationship, love, and respect" as known in Jesus (61). The words reflect the idea of human beings as tools, objects, or commodities that God uses to perform a task. Rather, Young explains that all people are God's children made in his image to be in relationship with him. He invites people to participate with him. Young concludes: "God is a God of relationship and never acts independently."

The Biblical Response

What Young says here flows from universal reconciliation (UR), which teaches that God is love and all that he does is loving. Young also assumes that all people are his children and all people are in relationship with God.

What is lacking throughout all UR literature is acknowledgement of God's other attributes of holiness, righteousness, and justice, which are equally and completely perfected in understanding the nature of God. The Bible clearly teaches that not all people are God's children. Indeed, no people are until they believe in Christ and receive him – as the texts cited in chapter 5 attest. Otherwise, people come short of God's glory and come under his judgment of an eternity separated from him (Romans 3:23; John 3:16-18). They need to be saved (Romans 3:26), as 1 Corinthians 6:9-11 also indicates:

> Do you not know that the wicked will not inherit the kingdom of God? Do not be deceived: Neither the sexually immoral nor idolaters nor adulterers nor male prostitutes nor homosexual offenders nor thieves nor the greedy nor drunkards nor slanderers nor swindlers will inherit the kingdom of God. And that is what some of you were. But you were washed, you were sanctified, you were justified in the name of the Lord Jesus Christ and by the Spirit of our God.

Finally, for Young to assert that God "never acts independently" is not true. If it were true, then God is dependent on his creation, and God ceases to be God. The Apostle Paul says that God has need of nothing: *The God who made the world and everything in it is the Lord of heaven and earth and does not live in temples built by hands. And he is not served by human hands, as if he needed anything, because he himself gives all men life and breath and everything else* (Acts 17:24-25). Isaiah 40 and 41 also express the strength, power, and majesty of God.

The following reflections show that Young is wrong in this assertion. Did not God act independently when he created the universe, including human beings? When he determined to bring the flood? Indeed, when he brings the devil and all humanity into judgment?

Young's concept of the power of words is laudable, but how does he justify how he often disregards, denies, or distorts God's words? Universal reconciliation rejects much of the content of the Old and New Testament.

What Young says about God not using human beings as tools would be above suspicion if he weren't always propagating his UR with its truncated understanding of God and his works. Young manipulates God's words to use God to his advantage to promote heretical ideas.

The "lie" of this chapter is basically a straw-man argument.

CHAPTER 8

"GOD IS MORE HE THAN SHE"

(*Lies*, chapter 7)

Summary

With this "lie," Young addresses the sexual identity of God as both female and male in his nature and says that people who are equally sexual have relationship with this God.

Young begins his chapter 7 by relating his mother's struggle with his portrayal of God as a black woman in *The Shack*. As a young nurse, Young's mother saved the life of a premature baby boy weighing one pound. This child grew up in an Anglican pastor's home and became a missionary. Many years later, this fellow interceded on behalf of Young to alleviate his mother's concerns about the imagery Young used to portray God, particularly as a black woman. Young makes two points:

1. God is not more male than he is female. All of humanity's sexual distinctions arise from "the very nature of God." The image of God in people is equally feminine and masculine. Young writes that the "feminine/masculine nature of God is a circle of relationship, a spectrum, not a polarity" (73).

2. Imagery "was never intended to define God; rather, imagery is the window through which we see aspects and facets" of the nature of God (74). Young claims that all kinds of imagery are used of God – feminine, masculine, animal, inanimate objects, etc.

The Biblical Response

As somewhat typical of all of Young's writings, he uses stories to gain sympathy from his readers for his theology. I believe that this borders on emotional manipulation. In any case, most Christian theologians assert that God is without sex, since God is a spirit being, as Jesus said in John 4:24. Only Jesus, the Son of God, became human (note 1 Timothy 2:6); that is, he became a man, as conceived by the Holy Spirit in the womb of Mary the virgin. The Old Testament occurrences of the seeming human appearances of God or the LORD to various people are theophanies, or appearances of God, and all are probably preincarnate appearances of Christ.

Thus, it is off base to assert that God by nature is masculine/feminine. This probably stems from Young's other presuppositions that all humanity is created "in God" and that Adam was conceived in Eternal Man's (Jesus's) womb as a baby, which he asserts in his novel *Eve*. Further, Young asserts that God's feminine/masculine nature is a "circle of relationship" in which human beings fully participate (73). On the face of it, it would seem difficult to have a "pure relationship" among people and a spirit being. Of course, our relationship is with Jesus Christ, the God-man, but Young is clearly asserting femaleness and maleness as the *nature* of God; he does not distinguish this relationship as being with the Son of God.

Interestingly, Young's terms, "circle of relationship" tied to God's "feminine/masculine nature," suggest that God is fully dependent on human beings for his nature to be fully expressed. Young is not referring here to the Trinity as self-sufficient. Thus, his language is either quite loose and sloppy or he intends to reduce God to a human-dependent being, thus denying God's eternality, transcendence, and self-sufficiency, which the Apostle Paul asserts in Acts 17:25.

Young's words also suggest that relationship with God involves sexuality. Truly, Paul Young has created a god in his own image. His attempt to rewrite biblical truth leads him into corners and cul-de-sacs that are both unbiblical and irrational. His foundation based in UR has made him a heretic of the first order.

Further, Young seeks to defend his imagery of using a woman to depict both God the Father and the Holy Spirit (who also is without sex) in *The Shack*. But his imagery goes beyond any biblical imagery when he depicts the entire Trinity as human beings. It is biblically permissible to portray Jesus Christ with human imagery, since he became and remains the God-man, but never does the Bible give allowance to portray the Father and Spirit along with the Son as three separate human beings; this violates the mystery of the Trinity as the Three-in-One. Such imagery violates the Second Commandment, forbidding the making of images to portray God.

But of course, for Paul Young the Bible holds little restraint on his imaginations.

The "lie" of this chapter is not only an error as Young has stated it, but he is also in error in his attempt to correct it by asserting that God is equally both "he" and "she."

CHAPTER 9

"GOD WANTS TO BE A PRIORITY"

(*Lies*, chapter 8)

Summary

Here Young asserts that speaking of having God as a priority is problematic because it suggests a magical idea. Young says that people are in a relationship with God where he is central. Young links the idea of God being a priority with people's magical expectation of God. People think that if they have the right formula of words, works, and faith to use with God, then they will get the right result. Failure to get results may be due to lack of prayer, faith, or some sin. The goal, he says, is "control, or at least certainty" (75).

Young advances to his topic about priority. He notes his discovery that the Greek of the New Testament does not have a word for either "priority" or "principle" – words that Christians often use. He addresses the particular text in which Jesus is asked which of the commandments is the "most important" (the translation of *megale*), and Jesus's answer is the commandment to love God with one's total being.

> *Hearing that Jesus had silenced the Sadducees, the Pharisees got together. One of them, an expert in the law, tested him with this question: "Teacher, which is the greatest command-ment in the Law?"*
>
> *Jesus replied: "'Love the Lord your God with all your heart and with all your soul and with all your mind.' This is the first*

and greatest commandment. And the second is like it: 'Love
your neighbor as yourself.' All the Law and the Prophets hang
on these two commandments." (Matthew 22:34-40)

This, Jesus says, is the *first* and *greatest* commandment. The Greek terms
are *megale* and *prote* (literally the order is *greatest* and *first*). Young
insists that these terms do not point to priority, what is first, but to what
is central. Young is out to make the point that the idea of first suggests
a list, and lists are "about control and performance," whereas "God is
about adventure and trust" and about "love and relationship." People
need to move from the "legalism of priorities and its inevitable guilt"
to developing relationships in which God is "central to everything"
(81-82). How we live in relationship and love with people rather than
according to duty and performance is how we should live with God.

The Biblical Response

Young presents the idea that people who seek to please God are seeking
"control" or "certainty." In this way, Young discounts priorities. This is
his typical way of dismissing any basis or credibility to the idea of obey-
ing God. Yet note that in the passage that Young brings forward about
the two greatest commandments, they are *commandments: You shall*
love. . . . Apparently, the idea of obedience and performance is okay in
loving, but is not okay in anything else that God tells us to do or obey.

The whole idea of "certainty" is offensive to Young. In *The Shack*, he
has Sarayu, representing the Holy Spirit, say that she delights in uncertainty (203). This is in line with Young's self-description as one who is
always asking questions. It seems that the only answers he accepts are
those that flow from his confession of universal reconciliation (UR),
while he rejects the Bible's answers.

The way that Young translates *prote* is questionable. The word does
not necessarily mean "foremost," but simply "first," as given above in
the translation. The same word occurs in Jesus's command to *seek first*
his kingdom and his righteousness (Matthew 6:33). Thus, Young's com-
plaint about the idea of *first* versus *central* lacks the punch he thinks
he finds in the Greek words. Further, for Jesus to say *love God* and *love*
your neighbor must include action to prove that one does love God

and others. Note that James 2:26 says that *faith without works is dead*; so, love without evidence of it is dead. While Christians should live in relationship with God, a "pure relationship" which Young espouses in *The Shack* is impossible (more about this in other chapters). Guidelines and boundaries are necessary for any relationship to succeed, whether with people or with God; otherwise, relationships may collapse on a whim and trust will be lost.

Again, Young tries to make much "hay" out of what the words of the New Testament mean, but he skirts his accountability to all the words – the teaching of the Bible as a whole. We only know authoritatively the Word revealed in human flesh as we discover him in the words of the Bible.

> *In the beginning was the Word, and the Word was with God, and the Word was God. He was with God in the beginning. Through him all things were made; without him nothing was made that has been made. In him was life, and that life was the light of men. The light shines in the darkness, but the darkness has not understood it.* (John 1:1-5)

Every Christian can appreciate the idea that God should be central in our relationship with him and not just a priority. Hence, this is basically a straw man that Young raises. However, the way that Young goes about defending this idea is pure UR with all of its hidden agendas, denials, and slander of God and the Bible.

CHAPTER 10

"GOD IS A MAGICIAN"

(*Lies*, chapter 9)

Summary

The idea of God being a magician was introduced in *Lies* chapter 8. Young builds on this idea in chapter 9 by showing that Christians use various means, like magic, to control God. He acknowledges that most religious people would deny that they believe that God is a magician. In certain ways, however, they show that they are resorting to magic – at least in the way Young describes magic.

By magic, Young refers to using certain means to "exert control over someone or something," a "power play" (83). What are these means? Young identifies them as the use of rituals, symbols, actions, and language with the "aim of exploiting power." He writes, "Behind religious magic is belief in a God who needs to be coerced to do something." If people do the right thing or "say the right prayer," then "God is obligated to respond in a certain way." But Young objects to this process. He asserts that God's response is motivated by love, not "by our performance or skill in prayer" (84).

The reason people resort to "magic" is that they "neither trust God's goodness nor God's love" (84). Young singles out two kinds of magic: faith-magic and performance-magic. The first kind means that one should be able to move mountains and do other special things, and when "something goes wrong" it is because the person did not have enough faith or exercised it improperly (85).

At this point Young tells the story of how much difference there was between his wife's family (outgoing, loving life, emotionally healthy) compared to his own (rigid, religious, "lied about most stuff"). Young goes on to illustrate his personal encounter with "faith-magic" (86-87).

Young next recounts an experience that seemingly shows the short-comings of the other kind of magic – "performance-magic." It involves doing "the right things," such as reading the Bible, attending church, tithing, praying, and going on mission trips (88). Doing these and other things will bring God's blessing.

The alternative to both kinds of magic is relationship, which involves "mystery and the loss of control" and trust. Young encourages his read-ers to pursue relationship, for in it people will hear the voice of God in their own "unique way of hearing." Participation in relationship is "where the real action is" (91-92).

The Biblical Response

Once again, Young resorts to his denunciation of performance in order to propagate his preference for relationship. It is one of the most fun-damental points of his universal reconciliation (UR), taking second place only to the assertion that God is love and love limits all his other attributes.

I believe that Young is in error in what he labels "magic," whether it is "faith-magic" or "performance-magic." There are probably hun-dreds of exhortations in the Bible to believe and trust God (such as in the Psalms) and to put faith in Christ. To Nicodemus, Jesus said, *You must be born again* (John 3:7). And there are hundreds of exhortations to obey God and our Lord Jesus Christ, as I pointed out earlier. The Great Commission in Matthew 28:18-20 is a clear example. Jesus said, *All authority in heaven and on earth has been given to me. Therefore go and make disciples of all nations, baptizing them in the name of the Father and of the Son and of the Holy Spirit, and teaching them to obey everything I have commanded you.*

The real issue is not what Young identifies, but that Christians would exercise faith and practice obedience for the right motives. Neither of these activities is done for oneself – to make oneself more holy. They are done for the glory of God and are accomplished by the enabling of the Holy Spirit.

What is wrong about Young's list of things in his "performance-magic" is that they all involve activities that the Bible either encourages or commands. They are the disciplines of the Christian life that are to make us more and more like our Savior and Lord. The Apostle Paul encouraged Timothy to *have nothing to do with godless myths and old wives' tales; rather, train yourself to be godly* (1 Timothy 4:7). Would Paul Young directly oppose what Jesus and the apostles tell us to do? By what authority does he do this?

I will say several times in this book that Paul Young's advocating of a relationship with God is beyond realization in the ways he describes. But he must say what he does because he has totally bought into the beliefs of UR that all people are already God's children; no one needs to be saved, since all already are; there is no judgment or no hell, because God is love. So the only thing left for people to do is to accept being children of God already and to exercise that in a deeper relationship with God.

It is interesting that Young would describe his family background as "lying." Young's confession may reveal a background that continues to influence his own habits and his frequent use of "lies" – as in the title of the present book under review, his chapter titles, and his continual mentioning of "lies." He uses the word eight times in chapter 13 in his novel *Cross Roads*. And note how he has failed to tell the whole truth regarding his embrace of universalism and his writing of *The Shack*, as I pointed out in the introduction at the beginning of this book.

The thrust of this chapter, "God is a magician," is a lie, of course. No mature Christian thinks of God this way – including the way that Young defines magic. It is a straw man.

CHAPTER 11

"GOD IS A PRUDE"

(*Lies*, chapter 10)

Summary

Paul Young takes up the issues of human sexuality and God's "sexuality." What he says about relationship with a sexual deity is alarming.

Here Young deals with a topic, namely sexuality, that in certain degrees was hush-hush among Christians. But the way Young deals with it is unbalanced; he says a few good and positive things, but then asserts some blasphemous things that far outweigh the positive things.

Young begins by asking the important question, "Where do you think sexuality originates?" He answers, "It originates in the very being of God" (93). But how Young understands this is quite disturbing and colors everything he says in this chapter – to which I'll return in my response that follows.

Young illustrates that sexuality is pervasive in culture, including the culture of tribes where Paul spent his childhood. It is not clear why Young tells this story, until we come to the last page of the chapter. Young asserts that sex, money, and power become despotic if not contained by love and relationship.

Young appeals to three Greek word studies in developing his view of sexuality:

1. He asserts that the New Testament tells us that "the divine nature of God has been placed within us," and the word for "nature" is *sperma*. Young adds: "Sexual union is 'knowing'

another, the intimacy of face-to-face oneness" (95). In light of what Young says elsewhere, his words here mean that all humanity has God's divine nature by virtue of having been created by God and in God.

2. The second Greek term that Young employs in his discussion of the sexuality of God is *perichoresis*, which he defines as "mutual interpenetration without loss of any individual Person." Young claims that the early church employed this term to describe the nature of the Trinity. I dispute this claim below. In any case, Young goes on to say that this is "one of the best descriptions of sexual union I've heard" (95). He then adds, "It celebrates that this attraction and drive exist because we are created in the image and likeness of God." These words raise serious concerns, as the previous point does for the same reason.

3. The third Greek term that Young deals with is *agape*, which means "love." All relationships must be grounded in this "other-centered, self-giving, committed love." Young says sexuality is "a beautiful and a creative force only when it is an expression of *agape*." The New Testament totally avoided using the classical word *eros*, from which we get the word *erotic*, because Eros was a pagan deity associated with "self-centered and self-servicing power" seeking "self-gratification" (such as in pornography) and a yearning for wholeness (as in infatuation) (95-96). The *eros* kind of love is totally at odds with biblical *agape*. Furthermore, Young adds, this biblical kind of love reveals how wrong pornography and infatuation are.

The Biblical Response

Regarding the first word study, Young is totally wrong in several ways. First, the New Testament never says that the "divine nature" has been "placed within" all humanity. The closest the Bible comes to this is 2 Peter 1:4 and 1 John 3:9:

> *Through these he has given us his very great and precious*

promises, so that through them you may participate in [par-take of] the divine nature. (2 Peter 1:4)

No one who is born of God will continue to sin, because God's seed remains in him; he cannot go on sinning, because he has been born of God. (1 John 3:9)

Neither writer says that the divine nature has been placed within Christians and certainly not in all humanity. Peter says that Christians have become partakers of or participants in the divine nature, not that the divine nature has been placed within people. Peter could never mean that Christians become divine in the sense that they become deities, having the same nature that God has. The word for "nature" is *physis*. No Jewish writer, such as Peter, could ever mean this. Rather, Peter means that Christians begin to exhibit the divine attributes that are communicable to and duplicated by human beings, such as love, patience, endurance, goodness, and mutual affection, as later verses in 2 Peter indicate:

For this very reason, make every effort to add to your faith goodness; and to goodness, knowledge; and to knowledge, self-control; and to self-control, perseverance; and to persever-ance, godliness; and to godliness, brotherly kindness; and to brotherly kindness, love. For if you possess these qualities in increasing measure, they will keep you from being ineffective and unproductive in your knowledge of our Lord Jesus Christ. (2 Peter 1:5-8)

It is a stretch to go from "partaking in the divine nature" to say that the "divine nature has been placed in all people." Young is making everyone a deity!

The Apostle Paul gives clarity here. He writes that Christians have been adopted into God's family by means of their faith:

For you did not receive the Spirit that makes you a slave again to fear, but you received the Spirit who brought about your adoption to sonship. And by him we cry, "Abba, Father." (Romans 8:15; also verse 23)

> *To redeem those under law, that we might receive adoption to sonship.* (Galatians 4:5)

In Roman culture, such an adoption meant that a person received equal, legal rights with all the actual, "real," natural-born children of a household. Thus, people who have believed in Christ, *sons of God through faith in Christ Jesus* (Galatians 3:26), are not the "real" children of God (God doesn't have babies), but are adopted into his family and reveal that they are such children by the way they live.

The other text, 1 John 3:9, says, *No one who is born of God will continue to sin, because God's seed* [here *sperma* is used] *remains in him; he cannot go on sinning, because he has been born of God.* Clearly, in this context John is writing to and about Christians who have been born again (1 John 2:29). John is contrasting the lifestyle of Christians, those born of God who are God's children, with the lifestyle of those not born of God who are children of the devil and keep on sinning and failing to do right.

> *No one who lives in him keeps on sinning. No one who continues to sin has either seen him or known him. Dear children, do not let anyone lead you astray. He who does what is right is righteous, just as he is righteous. He who does what is sinful is of the devil, because the devil has been sinning from the beginning. The reason the Son of God appeared was to destroy the devil's work. No one who is born of God will continue to sin, because God's seed remains in him; he cannot go on sinning, because he has been born of God. This is how we know who the children of God are and who the children of the devil are: Anyone who does not do what is right is not a child of God; nor is anyone who does not love his brother.* (1 John 3:6-10)

John makes his point quite explicitly when he says, *Everyone who believes that Jesus is the Christ is born of God* (1 John 5:1).

Thus, Young is wrong to assert that all humanity is involved and that deity is being placed in people. Rather, Christians reveal certain divine qualities due to being born again; they reveal their Father in their character.

The second fallacy in regard to divine nature that Young promotes occurs when he talks about "us," or all humanity. His universal reconciliation (UR) belief asserts that all humanity is already saved, all people are already children of God, and from birth all are on the continuum of faith. But Peter, Paul, and John write about Christians partaking of the divine nature when describing the transformation of some people by faith. These apostles are addressing people who had been lost in unbelief, but now they are believers. Young treats people as always having been born of God; they never were otherwise.

The third fallacy is that Young seems to equate "sexual union" with "knowing another," and he carries this to the relationship that people have with God – the "intimacy of face-to-face oneness" (95). These are Young's special words to describe the relationship with God. They occur repeatedly in his novel *Eve* and in chapter 24 of *Lies* to describe how all humanity is already in Christ; all are saved; all are in God.

Thus, it appears that Young is asserting that human beings are in sexual union with God, since sexuality is part of the divine nature that God "has placed within us" – all humanity. And all are in "relationship" with him, knowing him sexually. Later Young says that "sexual intimacy" is the "stunning expression" of our bearing the image of God (96).

In response to the second Greek term (*perichoresis*) that Young uses, he seems to be reinforcing his belief that God is a sexual being and that there is sexual interpenetration within the Godhead! He says that humans are sexual beings because they are created in God's "image and likeness" (95). Yet the New Testament, the early church, and Jewish and Christian theology have never asserted that God is a sexual being. He is spirit (John 4:24). The Bible makes it clear that humans were created, among other reasons, as sexual beings for the primary purpose of procreation – to have babies. Genesis 1:28 says, *Be fruitful and multiply and fill the earth* (ESV). Jesus seems to assert that angels, who are also spirit beings, are not sexual beings and do not procreate to have baby angels. He says, *At the resurrection people will neither marry nor be given in marriage; they will be like the angels in heaven* (Matthew 22:30).

Young appeals to the Greek word *perichoresis*, defining it as "mutual interpenetration without loss of any individual Person." He claims that it was used by the early church to describe the Trinity. My research finds that Young's statement misrepresents the truth in several ways.

1. The word may be only general in nature, meaning "interchange."

2. The word never occurs in the New Testament.

3. The word occurs in the works of only two church fathers in reference to the idea of "interpenetration within the Trinity": Cyril of Alexandria (died in 444) and John of Damascus (died in 749).

4. This is a relatively later dating for early church fathers. These are not the apostolic fathers – the earliest church fathers – who repeatedly affirm what evangelicals believe today regarding the judgment of the wicked in an everlasting hell.[22]

5. These two fathers use this term quite infrequently (six times): Cyril uses the noun form of it only one time and John of Damascus five times.

6. These same two fathers may use it for the general idea of "interpenetration" an additional ten times or so. They also use the verb form a similarly limited number of times.

Thus, what Young would have us believe about usage by the early church turns out to be in exceedingly few cases, dated relatively late in time as far as the early church is concerned, and limited to two church fathers (mainly one). This hardly represents significant usage and should contribute little in understanding the nature of the Triune God.

Also, on a website, Young recently appealed to the works of the church father Athanasius and to the Nicene Creed to support his claim that he is not a heretic and that he is orthodox in his theology.[23] In appendices 1 and 2, I weigh this claim by examining the Nicene Creed and the teachings of Athanasius and find that the claim is in error.

Regarding the third Greek word to which Young appeals, *agape,*

---

22 See my forthcoming book on the fallacies of universal reconciliation, where I devote an entire chapter to show that the early church fathers almost unanimously speak of salvation and future judgment very much in line with how evangelical doctrine expresses these same matters today.

23 In an interview ("William Paul Young: Orthodox Novelist," posted Feb. 28, 2017) recorded on the website of C. Baxter Kruger, called "Perichoresis."

he does better. Following the Greek Old Testament (the LXX – the Septuagint), the New Testament used a word of relative obscurity to describe the kind of love that God has for us and that we should have for others. Young correctly condemns pornography and infatuation as violating this kind of love. These are based in "an imaginary relationship" and are the opposite of "knowing" (96). He finds that romance, sexual intimacy, and sensuality are consistent with *agape* love (I would add, and I hope he would, "when they are exercised within marriage").

Although the New Testament uses of *agape* love predominately have nothing to do with sexuality, Young repeatedly brings up sexuality in his discussion, so perhaps love almost always has sexual connotations for Young, at least indirectly. Since he says sexuality is part of God's nature and all people are in an intimate relationship with God, knowing him sexually seems to be a given for Young. Note this section that again brings sexuality to the fore (97):

"What if *agape* is the ground of all authentic face-to-face intimacy, sexual and otherwise, and is a celebration of the flow of other-centered, self-giving love? Then knowing and being known make sense, and the depths of authentic relationship become essential to sexual expression. . . . [Self-giving love] is mutual interpenetration without the loss of individual personhood (*perichoresis*)."

On the last page of this chapter, we find out why Young cited the clothing-less tribe among whom he grew up. He remarks that for them, "human sexuality is a good and right language of intimacy" (98). Yet Young makes no mention of the shame of nakedness that our first parents brought to the race of human beings – shame caused by the guilt of sin (Genesis 3). It is shame that God recognized and disapproved when he clothed Adam and Eve. Nakedness outside of marriage continues to be shameful.[24]

But of course, here again Young has no regard for the authority of

---

24   All kinds of references bear this out, especially in the Old Testament. It is often used symbolically, used to represent "nothing" or destitution; it is most frequently used in connection with all kinds of sexual sins (Lev. 18, 20). In the New Testament Jesus uses it several times in his parable of the sheep and the goats (Matt. 25:31-46) as something to be covered; it is a sign of spiritual destitution (Rev. 3:17); it is something (shame?) that cannot separate the Christian from God (Rom. 8:35). It is often associated with shame (1 Sam. 20:30; Isa. 47:3; Mic. 1:11; Rev. 3:18), and probably should always be inferred. Significantly, Jesus died on the cross scorning its shame (Heb. 12:2).

the Bible in guiding our understanding of humanity and of God – and of sexuality.

Here, again, Young has constructed a straw man. But in the process of tearing down what he believes to be a "lie," he goes to the extent of slandering God by apparently making God into a sexual being with whom we engage in relationship.

CHAPTER 12

"GOD BLESSES MY POLITICS"

(*Lies*, chapter 11)

Summary

In his chapter 11, Young takes up both the institution of government and the politics connected to it. He shares what his own attitude is toward war and killing and his involvement in it.

Paul Young addresses a topic – the institution of government – about which he expressed very strong words of denunciation in *The Shack*. He said that government is one of a demonic "trinity of terrors [along with the institutions of the church and marriage] that ravages the earth" and that man, not God, created it (*The Shack,* 122-124, 179). The film *The Shack* had little, if any, dialogue about government. Has Young softened his attitude toward government? Not really. In addition, we learn why Young would never take up a gun in combat.

Young reveals that he holds dual citizenship in Canada and the US. But the dual citizenship that he discusses concerns the mixing of religion with politics, nationalism, and patriotism. He faults the use of biblical prophecy to justify our nationalistic tendencies. Maturity for some Christians means that they find that their "version of god was actually a local deity," and this concept was used to justify violence and the rewriting of history according to the winners' ideas. Young especially laments the loss of life and limb by many in support of "local, political deities" (101).

Even though Young unfortunately projects a negative attitude toward government, there are more serious concerns that Young's statements raise:

1. In several ways Young asserts that human beings, not God, "originated or instituted" government in order to bring about "security and certainty" (102).

2. Government is obviously broken. Politics is not a solution.

3. Government, but not God, is about separation, division, domination, and power.

4. The kingdom of God has no political alliances or agenda and is in tension with the kingdoms of this world.

5. Young finds the "roots" of "political power" in Cain's murder of his brother in Genesis 4 (103).

6. Every nation exists "because of the bloodshed of brothers," which Young calls "murder" (104).

7. Young commits himself to "peaceful resistance" and the kingdom of God, where violence is never appropriate, but "turning the other cheek" is appropriate (105).

The Biblical Response

Every Christian can acknowledge that governments, past and present, have often failed and are often in conflict with Christ's kingdom, but it is not necessary to misrepresent the biblical foundation and purpose of earthly kingdoms.

Regarding point 1, it is God who has established all governments and nation states, and the Apostles Paul and Peter strongly argue this fact:

> *From one man he made every nation of men, that they should inhabit the whole earth; and he determined the times set for them and the exact places where they should live* (Acts 17:26).

> *Everyone must submit himself to the governing authorities, for there is no authority except that which God has established.*

> *The authorities that exist have been established by God.*
> *Consequently, he who rebels against the authority is rebel-*
> *ling against what God has instituted, and those who do so will*
> *bring judgment on themselves* (Romans 13:1-2).

> *Submit yourselves for the Lord's sake to every authority insti-*
> *tuted among men: whether to the king, as the supreme author-*
> *ity, or to governors, who are sent by him to punish those who do*
> *wrong and to commend those who do right* (1 Peter 2:13-14).

Also, Genesis 10 and 11 reveal that the beginning of governments or nations goes back to the time just after the flood and the Tower of Babel. Contrary to the fifth point above, Cain's murder of Abel was not the beginning of nations, nor was the work of Enoch and Lamech the beginning. Young is in error to make the formation of governments man's idea rather than God's.

Consider also that God's reign on earth was to be through Israel, then through Israel's kings, and now through the kingdom of Messiah. The latter is now here in certain respects, but will be more fully realized in the millennial age. The full realization of Messiah's kingdom could hardly have any negative aspects. But of course, Young has no future, millennial kingdom.

Regarding points 2 through 4 above, the kingdoms of earth could never be a match for the integrity and ethics of the kingdom of God. However, the opposite – having no governments or nation states – would be far worse, for then anarchy, chaos, and greater evil would prevail.

It is typical for pacifists, as seen in points 6 and 7, who embrace "peaceful resistance" to identify armed killing in battle as "murder," but thankfully enough people recognize the difference between personal, "pre-meditated murder" of an individual and terrorism and fighting in battle – a nation's self-defense.

Christians have largely supported the death penalty exercised by the state as a necessary action by the state when someone murders a person made in the image of God. Pacifists trumpet "turning the other cheek," but this ethic from the Sermon on the Mount was never intended for nations, but only for individuals.

Young totally overlooks several factors. Some nations are more righteous or just in their conduct than others. In World War II, Hitler's Germany embraced a factor of evil far greater than the Allies did. Currently, terrorism exercised by ISIS and others in the name of Islam is a far greater evil.

Another factor is this. It was Christians, not pagans, who began formulating "just-war criteria" as early as Augustine in the fifth century. These criteria have been largely embraced by nations in the West. They include refusal to strike first, proportionate and measured response, and avoidance of harming civilians.

Young also fails to recognize the relationship of law, morality, and faith or religion. It is the faith of a people that determines their morality, and this in turn determines the legislation or laws of a country. If Christians don't strongly exercise their faith and the resulting morality, someone else's laws will be enacted.

Finally, Jesus himself recognized the existence of pagan and secular authority in governments and their necessary existence side-by-side with God's kingdom. His statement, *Render to Caesar the things that are Caesar's, and to God the things that are God's* (Matthew 22:21 ESV), forms the greatest principle for the relation of God's kingdom to man's in the history of mankind. As I've written elsewhere, our constitutional republic rests heavily on this principle.[25]

Obviously, Paul Young's concept of relationship runs counter to the idea of kingdom. One wonders why he even embraces the idea of the kingdom of God, since in his pure relationship there is no authority or submission. Is he not being inconsistent?

One other thing is important. Young's strong anti-government position recalls the strong anti-institution position of *The Shack*. As shown by the preceding discussion, this chapter continues the same perspective. Contrary to Young, government, marriage, and the church were originated by God, not by the devil.

---

25 For a more complete discussion of government and the principles that should guide Christians in their relationship to it, read my *To Submit or to Rebel against the State? Seven Biblical Principles to Guide Christians Everywhere During an Age of Revolution and in the Struggle for Religious Freedom* (Eugene, OR: Wipf & Stock, 2012). I discuss just-war criteria in chapter 5; the influence of Christ in chapter 6; the relationship of faith, morality, and law in chapter 8; and in an appendix, I quote the views of the Reformers on church and state.

This "lie" of Young's chapter 11 is basically a straw man in the way that Young has stated it. There is much more about the Christian's relation to the state that needed to be said.

CHAPTER 13

"GOD IS NOT GOOD"

(*Lies*, chapter 16)

Summary

In his sixteenth chapter, Young takes up the universal questions: "If God is good, why do I suffer? Why is there so much evil in the world?" He tries to answer these from the standpoint of universal reconciliation (UR), but not from the Bible.

Young begins by addressing what people mean when they say, "God is Good, all the time! All the time, God is Good!" He suggests that in spite of this greeting, the "lie," "God is not good" creeps in, and people question the goodness of God.

True to his pattern in virtually every chapter, Young turns to an illustration that emphasizes the point of his chapter. As the key for, or basis of, resolving theological challenges, he appeals to emotion and reason.

Young cites the example of a woman who is in continuous pain, whose child also lives in chronic pain. She is angry at Christian authors who don't write about the kind of pain she experiences and make everything turn out well by the end of the story. She asked Young if his writing would have the same content if he were writing out of pain.

Young answers that "of course" his books would look different (143). He thinks that her anger at Christian authors is justified, but on his way to this answer, he cites how he tried to deal with these issues in his novels *Eve* and *The Shack*, but in them such issues still needed to be resolved. Young appeals to his own experiences of pain and observes that "this world is not all there is, and death is not the definer or solution" (144). He goes on: "The existence of evil is a wrenching question," but then he says that the "greater philosophical/theological question is why any Good exists at all" (145).

Young appeals to the fact that God is the source of Good and Light, and "if God is not Good all the time, then trust is a delusion, and we are left truly alone in a world of hurt" (145-146). The suffering and pain can "blind" people to the Good all around, to the "grace that is constantly poured out," and the "life and light that push away the illusion of darkness" (146). Even in the midst of great tragedies, there is a "solid rock, a place to stand, a profound agreement and potent declaration of trust that we can make, even if it only feels like barely a toehold" (146). Young repeats what he said at the very beginning: "God is Good, all the time! All the time, God is Good!" (146).

And this is where Young ends. It is all he has to say in response to the great questions he raised.

The Biblical Response

It should not escape our attention that chapter 2 of *Lies* ("God is good. I am not") said just the opposite of the title of this chapter 16. Obviously, both cannot be "lies," but it seems that Young wanted to return to the topic to address it once again. He says that people think they believe that God is good, but they secretly deny this when pain or tragedy strikes.

Young's discussion leaves much to be desired. Do you know what it is? It almost seems that here and in his novels, Young is at a loss to deal with the problem of evil and the question of the goodness of God. He seems almost desperate. He said it is a "wrenching question" (145).

Actually, Young's answer is quite shallow. Only in the most general way does his answer embrace the great help available in the Bible. Why does he not cite the great texts, such as Romans 8:28-39? This comforting passage ends with:

> For I am convinced that neither death nor life, neither angels
> nor demons, neither the present nor the future, nor any pow-
> ers, neither height nor depth, nor anything else in all creation,

will be able to separate us from the love of God that is in
Christ Jesus our Lord. (Romans 8:38-39)

Why not cite the many portions of the Psalms that deal with suffering and the presence of evil in the world, such as Psalm 27 where David declares his heart will not fear or Psalm 37 where he affirms his trust in the Lord? In Psalm 62 David proclaims God to be his rock and salvation, and in Psalm 97 he looks to the righteous reign of the Lord. Why not cite these words of encouragement for those who suffer?

Why not cite the great stories of tragedy in the Bible: the pilgrimage of Abraham, the struggles of his descendants Isaac and Jacob, the betrayal of Joseph at the hands of his brothers? What about the great book of Job that deals with these sorts of questions in their entirety? Then there is the greatest story of all, the life and ministry of our Lord Jesus Christ. Jesus repeatedly went to the Old Testament to understand his own calling and to deal with temptation and suffering. Consider the afflictions suffered by the Apostle Paul, as recorded in the book of Acts and in 2 Corinthians (I deal with this issue of biblical encouragement in chapter 1 of *Burning Down the Shack*).

Perhaps Paul Young doesn't go to Scripture because for him the Bible takes second place to the influence of UR. Apparently the Bible is no longer the source of belief and understanding for him that it once was in his youth. He identifies himself as "questioning everything," including God. Why not trust, as we are exhorted in the Bible?

There are a couple more concerns. Does the answer to the problem of suffering and evil escape Young because he has "escaped" from the record of the Bible? In *Lies*, chapters 2 and 27, he rejects the fact of the fall into sin and the separation from God that began in the garden of Eden (as is made clear in his novel *Eve*) and brought the race of humanity into depravity and separation from God. He rejects the earlier fall of Satan into sin and rejects him as the one who tempts Adam and Eve to sin and who tempts Jesus to sin. He rejects the fall and the corruption of humanity that explain the power of the great perpetrators of evil on the stage of history.

Christians know the end of the story – that Jesus will return and put down evil and that all creation will be delivered from its bondage

(Romans 8). The eternal destiny for Christians is heaven and the presence of Jesus and the Father, where all suffering, sorrow, pain, and death are no more.

> *Do not let your hearts be troubled. Trust in God; trust also in me. In my Father's house are many rooms; if it were not so, I would have told you. I am going there to prepare a place for you. And if I go and prepare a place for you, I will come back and take you to be with me that you also may be where I am.* (John 14:1-3)

> *And I heard a loud voice from the throne saying, "Now the dwelling of God is with men, and he will live with them. They will be his people, and God himself will be with them and be their God. He will wipe every tear from their eyes. There will be no more death or mourning or crying or pain, for the old order of things has passed away.* (Revelation 21:3-4)

The end of the story needs to be dragged forward into each of our stories.

Without these realities, it is hard to explain the enormity of sin and evil. But this is just what UR does by its assertion that God is primarily love and good, and that people are not lost and in need of a savior. With this unreality as one's worldview, it is hard to deal with the harsher realities of life.

Young also uses capitals for *Good* and *Love* in these chapters. This suggests that Young is deifying these abstracts. He never uses terms like *just* and *righteous* to describe God.

Because Young has a truncated view of God, his view of evil is truncated. Note that he calls suffering an "illusion of darkness" (146). For all of humanity, suffering is not an illusion. Darkness is not an illusion. Suffering is real because evil is real. Jesus considered evil an essential part of reality during the present age. Note the temptation in the wilderness in Matthew 4, where Jesus rebukes the devil. The Apostle Paul had similar thoughts of resisting the devil:

> *The God of peace will soon crush Satan under your feet. The grace of our Lord Jesus be with you.* (Romans 16:20)

> *Put on the full armor of God so that you can take your stand*

against the devil's schemes. For our struggle is not against flesh and blood, but against the rulers, against the authorities, against the powers of this dark world and against the spiritual forces of evil in the heavenly realms. Therefore put on the full armor of God, so that when the day of evil comes, you may be able to stand your ground, and after you have done every-thing, to stand. (Ephesians 6:11-13)

Thus it is that Young's way of helping people in distress is truncated and an illusion. This "lie" is a straw man. No Christian informed by the Bible would believe that God is not good.

CHAPTER 14

"GOD IS A DIVINE SANTA CLAUS"

(*Lies*, chapter 20)

Summary

Young cites Brian McLaren, a fellow traveler in universal reconciliation (UR), as saying that every "authentic move toward God has to go through atheism" (173). Young takes this to mean that as people go through a crisis or other experiences, their understanding of God develops and faulty perceptions fall away.

Young takes up the idea that many people project their childhood conception of Santa Claus into their thinking about God (174). He says all have "misguided and often incoherent views of God" (174). Some see Jesus as the "Nice Santa God" who is delightful and pleasant, but who also expects good behavior (174-175). Others see God the Father as the "Nasty Santa God" who "requires perfect performance and morality" (176). Those who have the former view are often motivated to gain reward from Jesus by performance or by behaving properly. Those holding the latter view will be rewarded for "righteous and holy" behavior. For those who are "bad," the end is "a lot worse than not getting presents" (176).

Young notes that neither God nor Christ is Santa Claus, and that Santa doesn't exist. He asserts that God the Father is not "a different sort of Person from Jesus the Son" (176). Childish notions that people have about God need to be rooted up, just as Mack does in Sarayu's garden in *The Shack*. Young writes: "As lies and false imaginations about God are exposed, so are the roots that are entwined in our thoughts about ourselves and about our neighbor" (177-178).

Young observes that no one can have a relationship with Santa Claus, because he does not exist; one cannot have a relationship with an idea (178). But people look through him as through a window to observe themselves, and in their misperceptions they imagine that they are looking at God.

Then Young comes to his main point. "To understand who God really is, you can begin looking at yourself, since you are made in God's image" (178). All the good qualities that people desire to be are qualities of God. While many of these qualities may not be in one's experience, they are still people's yearning and desire.

Young then says that it is even better to look at Jesus, the incarnation of the "character and nature of God" (178-179). Young observes that as people "stumble toward the Light and Life of the goodness of God," their need for imaginary substitutes like Santa Claus fades. He concludes that "Real life, even in its suffering, is much more deeply rewarding than imagined life" (179).

The Biblical Response

Generally, Young does well when he writes that people need to move beyond their imaginations of God that are projections from how they view Santa Claus. He is correct to say that God the Father and Jesus the Son are not different sorts of Persons.

Yet, in light of Young's UR background, several concerns arise:

(1) For Young to encourage people to understand who God is by beginning to look at themselves fits Young's repeated attempt to make God in his own or man's image. The idea that the qualities people find in themselves match qualities in God assumes that people inherently have them, and this agrees with Young's basic assumption that people bear the *nature* (not just the image) of God. Bearing the nature of God means that they are divine, yet the Bible says that people are sinners by nature. Any divine qualities that reside in them are not due to human nature, but to the working of God directly or indirectly in them.

(2) Further, the Bible tells people to look not to themselves, but to Jesus Christ, *the author and finisher of the faith* (Hebrews 12:2). He is the supreme example and representative human being.

> First he said, "Sacrifices and offerings, burnt offerings and sin offerings you did not desire, nor were you pleased with them: (although the law required them to be made). Then he said, "Here I am, I have come to do your will." He sets aside the first to establish the second. And by that will, we have been made holy through the sacrifice of the body of Jesus Christ once for all. (Hebrews 10:8-10)
>
> To this you were called, because Christ suffered for you, leaving you an example, that you should follow in his steps. (1 Peter 2:11)

He is the only one to bear "the character and nature of God" in human flesh. John says God cannot be seen, but he is revealed in Jesus Christ: *No one has ever seen God, but God the One and Only, who is at the Father's side, has made him known* (John 1:18).

Nowhere in the Bible are we told to look at ourselves to find the standard by which to be or to live. Rather, we are exhorted to look at Jesus Christ finally and exclusively. Young says what he does because he believes that people are "fundamentally good" (see *Lies*, chapter 2), a belief that flows from UR.

As I have said before, virtually all of what Young believes and writes arises from his commitment, not to the Bible, but to universal reconciliation.

(3) For Young to admit that people cannot have a relationship with an idea ought to be taken to heart. Young's deep commitment to the idea of UR suggests that he has placed this idea above a personal experience with Jesus Christ as described in the Bible. Since he puts UR above the Bible (as measured by how often he falls in step with UR and virtually ignores the Bible), has he not fallen in love with an idea?

At this point it is legitimate to ask: Is this not how all cultic movements begin? A charismatic leader puts foreign ideas above the Bible's clear teaching.

(4) Once again, Young suggests that his understanding of UR is correct and should replace "the lies and false imaginations" that people have (177). Note his use of the word *lies* – a reference to the title of his book.

The "lie" that Paul Young identifies in chapter 20 is, of course, a straw man. But Young's greater aim is to label traditional beliefs about God, sin, forgiveness, and judgment (see *The Shack* and his other novels) and having a biblical relationship with God as "lies and false imaginations." It is astounding how consistently Young attacks biblical truth.

CHAPTER 15

"GOD IS NOT INVOLVED IN MY SUFFERING"

(*Lies*, chapter 22)

Summary

Young discusses the relationship of love (God) and suffering, and finds that for the present time they are inextricably connected. He says that all humanity has been resurrected in Christ to experience love and life.

Following his commitment to universal reconciliation (UR), Young finds it necessary to speak of the universality of all humanity as raised in the resurrection of Jesus Christ.

This chapter asks whether God is involved in all suffering, and the answer, contrary to the "lie" of the chapter's title, is yes. With illustrations from others and from himself, Young shows that suffering is the common lot of humanity. In this present world, love and suffering with its loss are intertwined. Suffering takes various forms.

1. Young is dealing with a slight revision of the question, "Can love exist without suffering?" By the incarnation, God joined humanity and experienced suffering.

As Young continues, several points stand out to me. He proceeds to show that suffering is not intrinsic to love, because prior to creation, love was expressed without suffering among the Godhead.

2. Adam introduced loss and suffering and death into the cosmos by his "independent turning from Life" (193).

3. Because people are "created in Christ, suffering was utterly embraced by God" (193).

4. "Because Jesus dwells within us as we are present to the hurts and losses of our broken world, we are participating with and in God (John 14:20)" (192-193).

5. God infuses "our suffering with Presence and Love" (193). Young relates the relationship of loss and suffering to the events of Easter.

6. Life reached out and pulled death into Life where it was "extinguished by Love. Saturday, in the valley of the shadow of death, Jesus plunders the place of the dead, and Resurrection morning raises all of humanity in His Life" (194). Thus, life springs out of death. Here, several features reflect Young's commitment to UR.

7. When people experience suffering, they are being invited to "be real and also to identify with humanity, and it is a fire that will burn away the false so that the true might emerge" (194-195). Young concludes the chapter by citing Mack's experience in *The Shack* and his own experience, how out of suffering he has been transformed to become more "free to love, to become more alive and human" (195).

8. Until death is fully eradicated, people in relationship with Jesus are growing in their participation in the suffering of others and "thereby participate in the abiding and active Love of God" (195).

The Biblical Response

Young deals here with a very important topic – the matter of suffering, how it relates to love, and the involvement of God in suffering. It is true that love prevailed among the Trinity prior to all creation, and that suffering for humanity came only with the fall. He also rightly draws attention to the meaning of Easter for settling the question of suffering and death. Yet even here, he resorts to the peculiar and unbiblical explanations that arise from UR.

Let me discuss points 1 and 5 first. Young equates love and God, as also shown in his other chapters. While this is true, it is characteristic of UR not to equate God with holiness, justice, and righteousness. These other attributes are just as frequently described as God's attributes as is love, and even more frequently with the death of Christ on the cross (Romans 3:23-26). It is more accurate to say that "God is love" than "love is God," for not all examples of love are divine (1 John 4:8, 16). In light of his UR viewpoint, however, Young probably means the latter.

The second point shows how Young characteristically describes "turning," what Christians call the fall of Adam and Eve into sin. By not calling it "sin" and "rebellion," UR softens it from the great evil that it is and negates the reason it cost God so much – the death of his Son. But the idea of "turning" predominates in his novel *Eve*. Also, it needs to be noted that Adam did not introduce suffering and death into the cosmos; Satan did. Adam introduced it into humanity as the result of Satan's temptation.

Why is it important to make this distinction? Because there was nothing in Adam to initiate temptation, for God had made him innocent and without a sin nature. Sin arose in Satan, and he solicited Adam to rebel against God. Universal reconciliation characteristically has little or no place for Satan, the devil, because his reality means that UR has to explain both his rebellion and his judgment in hell and his subsequent repentance to get out of hell. UR asserts that even the devil and the fallen angels will repent after suffering in hell and will enter into heaven. In *Burning Down the Shack* I show how such repentance is impossible from both a biblical and a rational standpoint (229-233). For one thing, such a belief makes heaven unsafe from additional, future rebellions of Satan.

In the third point, Young is apparently referring to the original creation of human beings in Christ, but may be thinking of the New Testament and all beings created in Christ (see also his *Lies*, chapter 3). *Therefore, if anyone is in Christ, he is a new creation; the old has gone, the new has come!* (2 Corinthians 5:17). Ephesians 2:10 adds to this with a purpose for us as new creations: *For we are God's workmanship, created in Christ Jesus to do good works, which God prepared in advance for us to do.* But by either account, all humanity is not created in Christ.

In Genesis, humans were not created in God nor in Christ but by God or by Christ. With the fact that Young states the identification of all humanity in Christ, he finds support to assert that all people have the divine nature (see similar teaching in *Lies*, chapter 10). If Young considered such Scriptures, he is in grave error, since only Christians, not all humanity, have been created in Christ Jesus to do good works (see my full defense of this in *Lies*, chapter 2).

Again, regarding point 4, only Christians participate with God in their reaching out to the suffering. Only believers have Christ dwelling within them. John clearly distinguishes between the followers of Christ and those of the world who will hate his disciples (John 14:17-23). Thus, not all humanity is in Christ, nor is he in them.

Regarding point 6 and the Easter events, death was defeated by Christ, not "extinguished," and it was by him, not by "Love." Furthermore, death was defeated only in the sense that he brought death to a judgment, which will be realized in actual life when Jesus comes again and reigns. To say that "Love" conquered death is the teaching of UR that makes the attribute of love limit all of God's other attributes. At the cross Jesus paid the price that justice and righteousness demanded for the weight of our sins in order to find forgiveness and remove our guilt (Romans 1:16-17; 3:23-26). To say that on Saturday "Jesus plundered the place of death" (note the avoidance of the term "hell") refers to UR teaching that Jesus went to hell between his death and resurrection to deliver repentant unbelievers from there. And if he could do it once, then he could go a "thousand times" to deliver people, as UR and Paul Young assert (as in his 2004 paper).

Finally, Young is in error to assert that on Resurrection Sunday Jesus raised "all humanity in His Life." Again, this is UR. The Bible says that only believers in Christ experience identification in Christ's death, burial, and resurrection, as described in Romans 6 and Colossians 2 (as I showed when discussing *Lies*, chapter 24).

What Christians celebrate as the capstone of their sacred celebrations, Easter, UR takes and distorts! There is nothing sacred and off-limits to UR.

Young's words in number 7 point to the meaning of suffering in hell according to UR, where the "purifying fires of suffering" will purge away all falseness so that truth may emerge. Such an idea is totally without biblical support. Compare instead how Jesus describes hell: everlasting darkness, where the worm does not die, torment, suffering, and such things. His apostles continue to reinforce his teaching (see my discussion in *Lies*, chapter 15).

The words of point 8 simply repeat the falsehood of point 4, but they could have been the occasion for Young to point to the future hope of Christians for deliverance when they are resurrected and reach their true home – where all suffering and death cease.

> *Brothers, we do not want you to be ignorant about those who fall asleep, or to grieve like the rest of men, who have no hope. We believe that Jesus died and rose again and so we believe that God will bring with Jesus those who have fallen asleep in him. According to the Lord's own word, we tell you that we who are still alive, who are left till the coming of the Lord, will certainly not precede those who have fallen asleep. For the Lord himself will come down from heaven, with a loud command, with the voice of the archangel and with the trumpet call of God, and the dead in Christ will rise first. After that, we who are still alive and are left will be caught up together with them in the clouds to meet the Lord in the air. And so we will be with the Lord forever. Therefore encourage each other with these words.* (1 Thessalonians 4:13-18)

> *Then I saw a new heaven and a new earth, for the first heaven and the first earth had passed away, and there was no longer any sea. I saw the Holy City, the new Jerusalem, coming down out of heaven from God, prepared as a bride beautifully dressed for her husband. And I heard a loud voice from the throne saying, "Now the dwelling of God is with men, and he will live with them. They will be his people, and God himself will be with them and be their God. He will wipe every tear from their eyes. There will be no more death or mourning or crying or pain, for the old order of things has passed away."* (Revelation 21:1-4)

First Corinthians 15, Hebrews 2:10-18, and John 14:1-3, 23 could also give hope to Christians, if Young had so desired to use those verses.

The "lie" of chapter 22 is truly a lie and thus a straw man. No Christian would assert that God is uninvolved in our suffering. In fact, many precious hymns remind us of the Lord's presence in all our suffering. Consider the words of "Day by Day":

> *Day by day and with each passing moment,*
> *Strength I find to meet my trials here;*
> *Trusting in my Father's wise bestowment,*
> *I've no cause for worry or for fear.*
> *He whose heart is kind beyond all measure*
> *Gives unto each day what He deems best –*
> *Lovingly, it's part of pain and pleasure,*
> *Mingling toil with peace and rest.*
>
> *Ev'ry day the Lord Himself is near me,*
> *With a special mercy for each hour;*
> *All my cares He fain would bear, and cheer me,*
> *He whose name is Counsellor and Pow'r.*
> *The protection of His child and treasure*
> *Is a charge that on Himself He laid:*
> *"As your days, your strength shall be in measure,"*
> *This the pledge to me He made.*
>
> *Help me then in every tribulation*
> *So to trust Your promises, O Lord,*
> *That I lose not faith's sweet consolation*
> *Offered me within Your holy Word.*
> *Help me, Lord, when toil and trouble meeting,*
> *E'er to take, as from a father's hand,*
> *One by one, the days, the moments fleeting,*
> *Till I reach the promised land.*

These words give the supreme source of the Christian's strength and peace in suffering.

CHAPTER 16

"YOU WILL NEVER FIND GOD IN A BOX"

(*Lies*, chapter 23)

Summary

Young deals with the idea of putting God in a box and why people do so. He redefines a "box" in which God may be.

In this chapter, Young deals with a popular topic – putting God in a box. He cites his personal experience of being in a religious box that had some helpful elements, some devastating ones to be unlearned, and some that seemed unfortunate earlier but later turned out to be good. Young seeks to illustrate the last category. He is largely autobiographical here.

Young identifies all kinds of boxes, both good and bad. He also describes these as categories (see the similar discussion in *Lies*, chapter 5 and elsewhere). He grew up in a "world of boxes" such as "worthy and unworthy, believer and unbeliever, saved and unsaved, and on and on" (199). While sometimes boxes are helpful (clarifying various types of diseases, for example), these religious kinds of categories are basically negative. Some boxes and categories can lead to "diabolical genocide and abuse," and some of these lead to "catastrophic things" done in the "name of God or humanism or plain old greed" (200).

Young acknowledges and appreciates that people have said that his writings have "helped them take God out of the box" (200), but he draws attention to the reality that when people leave one box, they may be tempted to "construct and climb into a new one" (200). Then they may arrogantly look down on those who are still in the boxes they have left. They may think that God has left with them, when he has stayed with the others. Also, people may think that they "could craft something, a box that can keep God out" (201). Young asserts that "whatever aspects of true freedom that have become a part of my life," they have always been attended by "a greater capacity to love, to accept, to enfold, to respect" (201).

Young concludes by citing what has become a profound discovery: "The only time we will find God in a box is because God wants to be where we are," and for Young, that is all the time (201).

The Biblical Response

It seems that this chapter is a twist on the saying, "You can't put God in a box." Young seems to assert that in spite of what people may do, God often joins (or remains with) people in a box of their creation. It seems that this chapter is a contrast for what Young said in his chapters 5 and 24, where he condemned spiritual categories such as "believer and unbeliever," "saved and unsaved." Here Young seems to say that God may still be with those who live in categories. He seems to correct his own overstatements. After all, how can one (Young) who rejects such categories or boxes do so without thinking of himself as in a better category or box? Isn't Young constructing a box or category? The answer is obvious.

I observe the following:

1. Young still condemns certain spiritual categories or boxes, yet these come from the Bible itself – from Jesus and the apostles. The Bible is our authority for thinking about "believers" and "unbelievers" (the perishing), "saved" and "unsaved" (John 3:16-18; Romans 10:9-10). Jesus thought in terms of those who were "born again" and those, such as Nicodemus, who yet needed to become such (John 3).

2. All such terminology is essential to preaching and believing the gospel.

3. While Young seems to take on a more humble approach to

categories, it is only a façade. Young asserts that he is correct in his condemnation of what the Bible approves, showing that he is still enmeshed in the beliefs of universal reconciliation (UR).

Note how Young's writing in this chapter evidences his commitment to UR. (a) Universal reconciliation claims that all people are God's children, all bear the divine nature, and all are already saved. Thus, categories are wrong. (b) Young's claim above to have found aspects of "true freedom" reflects what he said in his 2004 paper – that his conversion to universal reconciliation has affected all of what he believes and has made him a more loving person. Note his claim above to be more loving. Thus, Young still thinks from a UR perspective. Since love limits all of God's other attributes, love should limit all the beliefs and actions of the followers of UR. With this commitment to UR, Young is wrong.

4. Confusion arises when we say that God is in a box and then is not in a box. Since God is everywhere, he is present everywhere – in all boxes. On the other hand, if by saying that God is in a box, we mean that God gives approval to what is in a box, we are wrong. God only approves what the Bible says he approves. Outside of his approval are all the beliefs of UR.

5. Finally, the most obvious fault of Young is that he and other adherents to UR have created the most painful and illegitimate box or category. They have erected UR based primarily on emotion and reason in opposition to the Bible and Christian doctrine and history. They are the ones who divide the church by promoting teachings and beliefs contrary to the Bible itself. What greater boxes could be created than those that heretics have erected?

The book of *Lies* is evidence of the evil disposition of a heart and mind committed to a box (UR) from which all sorts of evil categories flow. Depending on whether a box is evil or good, the "lie" of this chapter is a distortion of the truth, or a half-truth. God will never be in a box approving evil.

CHAPTER 17

"GOD IS DISAPPOINTED IN ME"

(*Lies*, chapter 25)

Summary

Young takes up the sense of disappointment that people often feel, and he assures them that God is not ever disappointed with them. He begins, as he often does, by writing autobiographically. He reflects on his childhood when he felt that his missionary parents were continually disappointed in him. He acknowledges that he has never resolved this with his father (210). He suffered verbal abuse, and from the tribe, sexual abuse. This brought shame and dissonance because of conflicting values and beliefs; lack of trust was inevitable, as was silence. Children find ways to survive, including violence, self-punishment, addiction, withdrawal, and death.

Many experience both disappointments and grief throughout life. Young asserts that grief is a healthy response to loss and is often expressed as regret. But disappointment "largely revolves around expectations and imagination" that are not realized (213). In contrast, Young asserts that God, in spite of the "lies" people may believe and in spite of "darkness" people have, is never disappointed in people. Young writes, God is "never disillusioned by you"; he is "never disappointed in you; God has no expectations" (214).

Young cites Psalm 22 to assert that Jesus identifies with people in their delusion that God has forsaken them when he cried out from the cross that God had forsaken him (Psalm 22:1). But Jesus came to assert that God had not turned his face from him (Psalm 22:24). Thus, Young concludes that "God does not do abandonment. We will never be powerful enough to make God's face turn from us. Because God knows us utterly and is with us always – *you* are never a disappointment" (215).

The Biblical Response.

The topic of disappointment is quite important and universal, and Young's own history illustrates how devastating it can be. Yet some observations reveal how Young is wrong on such an important topic.

(1) Young seems to overlook the more significant aspect of disappointment. It is not so much that we believers will never be a disappointment to God or that he will never be disappointed in us, but the important truth is that God will never be a disappointment to us. The more transcendent truth is the reliability of God: he will never deny himself and will never go back on his promise. God will never violate his covenant, including the Abrahamic, Mosaic, and Davidic covenants, but especially the New Covenant that Jesus inaugurated at and by his death. The Lord's Supper is the commemoration of this New Covenant. We reaffirm our trust in God to keep his promise till Jesus returns (1 Corinthians 11).

(2) Young is a great disappointment in passing over the faithfulness of God. He places an emphasis on people and how they feel rather than on God who keeps his word. His word, his promise, is located in his written word, the Bible. These divine words, not the words of a novelist who violates the teaching of the Bible, provide relief for the saints.

(3) To affirm to all people that God is never disappointed in them is false. According to the Bible, God has shown grace to all, giving the life of his Son as an atonement for the sin of the world. *He is the atoning sacrifice for our sins, and not only for ours but also for the sins of the whole world* (1 John 2:2). *This is love: not that we loved God, but that he loved us and sent his Son as an atoning sacrifice for our sins* (1 John 4:10). God holds people responsible to believe the gospel and receive his

Son. To fail to do so means that people are choosing death and judgment over life and forgiveness (John 3:16).

(4) Contrary to Young, God does have expectations to which people should respond. God wants/wishes all to believe. *This is good, and pleases God our Savior, who wants all men to be saved and to come to a knowledge of the truth*, but he respects the choice of people to refuse to respond (1 Timothy 2:3-4). Failure to respond does not disappoint God, for he knew who would and would not respond. Nothing is in contradiction to God's perfect knowledge. Yet nonresponse means a rejection of him, and the consequences of this are real – everlasting judgment.

(5) Young's citation of Psalm 22 is inaccurate. The Psalm is about Jesus Christ and how when he became sin, God the Father for a short time abandoned him on the cross. The Psalm has nothing to do with God's disappointment of Jesus or Jesus's feeling such. Just the opposite is true. God was pleased with his beloved Son's work. Because the redemption of humanity was in the balance, God was *pleased to bruise him* (Isaiah 53:10 KJV). Jesus delighted to do God's will even if it meant being separated for a brief time, as he became sin and bore the judgment for it.

> *Yet it was the LORD's will to crush him and cause him to suffer, and though the LORD makes his life a guilt offering, he will see his offspring and prolong his days, and the will of the LORD will prosper in his hand.* (Isaiah 53:10)

> *Then he said, "Here I am, I have come to do your will." He sets aside the first [covenant] to establish the second [covenant]. And by that will, we have been made holy through the sacrifice of the body of Jesus Christ once for all.* (Hebrews 10:9-10)

God *was pleased* to make possible the reconciliation of the world through Christ if people believe:

> *For God was pleased to have all his fullness dwell in him, and through him to reconcile to himself all things, whether things on earth or things in heaven, by making peace through his blood, shed on the cross. Once you were alienated from God*

*and were enemies in your minds because of your evil behav-
ior. But now he has reconciled you by Christ's physical body
through death to present you holy in his sight, without blemish and free from accusation – if you continue in your faith,
established and firm, not moved from the hope held out in the
gospel.* (Colossians 1:19-23)

But of course, universal reconciliation (UR) rejects this central pillar
of the gospel – that Jesus came to save those who would respond to it
and accept it and believe that Jesus died for them.

(6) Further, Young is inconsistent again here. If UR is true, that all
people are already his children, why would there ever be a person in
whom God is disappointed?

(7) Also, this whole discussion flows from Young's belief in UR. There
is no biblical basis for Young to assert that God "delights" in all people,
and he is "with them always." This is universalist thinking. The Bible
says that he delights only in those who confess his Son as Savior, that
he will never leave them – those who are believers. Psalm 37:4 says,
*Delight yourself in the LORD and he will give you the desires of your
heart.* Hebrews 13:5-6 explains this further: *Keep your lives free from
the love of money and be content with what you have, because God has
said, "Never will I leave you; never will I forsake you." So we say with
confidence, "The Lord is my helper; I will not be afraid. What can man
do to me?"* There are no promises of blessings to those who are not born
again. In the Great Commission, Jesus promises to be forever with those
who preach and believe the gospel (Matthew 28:18-20).

(8) Repeatedly, Young refers to "lies" in this chapter and to "delusions"
and "imaginations." These terms recall the title of his book. Implicitly,
Young is asserting that evangelical faith, which would seek to save the
lost, is wrong. But he is the one who is in error. He holds out to lost
humanity a false hope that all is right between them and God, when
all is not.

This whole chapter is an effort in futility. There is no peace, no hope, no salvation, and no sense of God's presence for those who reject him. It may be that the feeling of disappointment and grief is God's way to bring people to an end of themselves so that they will cry out to God to save them, in spite of what Young writes here. The feeling of disappointment may be the work of the Spirit to bring conviction of sin (John 16:8-11).

Thus, the chapter's title, "God is disappointed in me," is both not a lie and a lie. It is the truth for those outside of Christ. In fact, his wrath is turned against those who don't believe. John 3:36 tells us that *whoever rejects the Son will not see life, for God's wrath remains on them.* Yet it is a "lie" for those who are truly God's children by new birth; and the greater truth is that God will never disappoint believers.

Note the encouraging words from the hymn, "What a Friend We Have in Jesus":

> *What a Friend we have in Jesus,*
> *All our sins and griefs to bear!*
> *What a privilege to carry*
> *Ev'rything to God in prayer!*
> *O what peace we often forfeit,*
> *O what needless pain we bear,*
> *All because we do not carry*
> *Ev'rything to God in prayer!*
>
> *Have we trials and temptations?*
> *Is there trouble anywhere?*
> *We should never be discouraged –*
> *Take it to the Lord in prayer.*
> *Can we find a friend so faithful*
> *Who will all our sorrows share?*
> *Jesus knows our ev'ry weakness –*
> *Take it to the Lord in prayer."*

CHAPTER 18

"GOD LOVES ME FOR MY POTENTIAL"

(*Lies*, chapter 26)

Summary

In this chapter, Young affirms that God loves people for who they are at any given point along life's course – not for what they might become.

Again, somewhat typically, Young writes autobiographically. He cites his early love for music and his significant achievement in playing the piano. But he couldn't read music, so he gave it all up when the pressure of others' expectations for his potential was too much for him to bear (218). In more recent years, Young has coached his children in some form of athletics, and he is now coaching his grandchildren. He finds that sports "offer an outlet for greater authenticity than many religious services," and there is an "honesty in sports" found in few other pursuits (219). But he acknowledges that sports also reveal the "darker side of humanity" where "fear of failure, low self-esteem" often surface. Fathers often link children's acceptability to their performance in sports, which is dependent on their "fulfilling their potential" (220-221).

Hence Young comes to the focus of this chapter. "Fulfilling your potential . . . is a moving target" usually determined by someone else (221). He asks, "Does God love me because of my potential? No!" (221). Human beings cannot enjoy their children in the present moment if their focus is on "some future potential that qualifies the value of each moment" (221).

At this point Young "corrects" the common reading of Proverbs

22:6 from *Train up a child in the way he should go* to "Train up a child in their way" – in each child's one-of-a-kind being (222).

Switching to the "lie" of this chapter, Young writes: "There is no end goal for us, no finally 'arriving,' no reaching the place of potential success. We are all eternal beings who are completely loved at every point along the way, and regardless of what our journey looks like, we are relentlessly loved inside every part of the process of this life" (222). He adds: "There is no 'potential' competition when it comes to being loved" (223).

The Biblical Response

Young makes some good observations about people's loves in life, and he recognizes how expectations of potential success may spoil people's best intentions for them. Yet when he applies this to spiritual matters, his universal reconciliation (UR) viewpoint comes through again.

(1) While in one sense God does not love us for our potential, in another sense he does indeed. God deeply and fully loves all genuine children of his who are born again, because he ultimately sees them as in his Son, as in Christ, and thus they are *holy in his sight, without blemish and free from accusation* (Colossians 1:22). He values them as fully complete and spiritually perfect because they are in Christ (Colossians 2:10).

Christians designate this as their position or standing, their essential identity – in Christ. Their daily living, their experience, may be much less than this perfection. Thus, Christians are to grow to maturity, to become knowledgeable in Christ and more holy in their daily living.

> *It was he who gave some to be apostles, some to be prophets, some to be evangelists, and some to be pastors and teachers, to prepare God's people for works of service, so that the body of Christ may be built up until we all reach unity in the faith and in the knowledge of the Son of God and become mature, attaining to the whole measure of the fullness of Christ. Then we will no longer be infants. . . . Instead, speaking the truth in love, we will in all things grow up into him who is the Head, that is, Christ.* (Ephesians 4:11-15)

Then one day, upon their passing into the presence of God, these Christians will be finally perfected in actuality. *Now we are children of God, and what we will be has not yet been made known. But we know that when he appears, we shall be like him, for we shall see him as he is. Everyone who has this hope in him purifies himself, just as he is pure* (1 John 3:2-3). *To him who is able to keep you from falling and to present you before his glorious presence without fault and with great joy* (Jude 24).

Besides our identity as perfect in Christ, and prior to the perfection that comes upon our entrance into his presence, God does love his children, imperfect though their living may be, all along the way. Romans 8:28-39 speaks to this, as does Jude 1: *Jude, a servant of Jesus Christ and a brother of James, To those who have been called, who are loved by God the Father and kept by Jesus Christ.* He will always remain faithful, for he tells us that *if we are faithless, he will remain faithful, for he cannot disown himself* (2 Timothy 2:13). But this is a wonderful, encouraging reality for those who are his genuine children. It is not true for all humanity, which is what Young, as a follower of universal reconciliation, believes.

(2) When Young seeks to retranslate Proverbs 22:6 from "the way" to "their way," he is embracing a later interpretation, even a modern one that flows from contemporary psychology. The context of Proverbs shows that there are only two ways: the way of the wise or righteousness and the way of the fool. The latter does not require discipline or training. The verse literally reads *his way* and refers to the way the young person should go. Virtually all translations take it as "the way." Young's view arises from universalism, which would reject "the way."

(3) Contrary to what Young says, there is an "end goal," a final "arriving," a "reaching" of "the place of potential success." The genuine people of God reach this goal when they pass on to glory to be forever with the Lord, whether by physical death or by the rapture: *When Christ, who is your life, appears, then you also will appear with him in glory* (Colossians 3:4). First Thessalonians 4:13-18 and John 14:1-3, which were cited earlier, also tell of the coming of Christ to receive his own.

The Apostle Paul had such a goal in mind as the focus of his daily living:

> *What is more, I consider everything a loss because of the surpassing worth of knowing Christ Jesus my Lord, for whose sake I have lost all things. I consider them rubbish, that I may gain Christ and be found in him, not having a righteousness of my own that comes from the law, but that which is through faith in Christ – the righteousness that comes from God on the basis of faith. I want to know Christ – yes, to know the power of his resurrection and participation in his sufferings, becoming like him in his death, and so, somehow, to attain to the resurrection from the dead. Not that I have already obtained all this, or have already been made perfect, but I press on to take hold of that for which Christ Jesus took hold of me. Brothers, I do not consider myself yet to have taken hold of it. But one thing I do: Forgetting what is behind and straining toward what is ahead, I press on toward the goal to win the prize for which God has called me heavenward in Christ Jesus.* (Philippians 3:8-14)

Young's words, "We are all eternal beings who are completely loved," are both true and false. The first half is true: all people live everlastingly. However, the Bible says that those who do not believe are lost, will perish everlastingly in judgment, and will experience the wrath of God (John 3:16-18, 36). These are not loved "along the way," as God's people are. They are not "completely loved." Young's UR is glaring here and in error.

So it seems that Young's "lie" here ("God loves me for my potential") is a half-truth and mostly a straw man. God fully loves his genuine children without any shadow, blemish, or defect.

CHAPTER 19

"GOD IS ONE ALONE"

(*Lies*, chapter 28)

Summary

Young rehearses how, out of his own broken experience, he came to write *The Shack*, and in so doing he has rejected the God he grew up with in his "modern evangelical Christian fundamentalism" (235-236).

Chapter 28 is Paul Young's final "lie." It is a fitting capstone to all of his lies and a fitting conclusion to this part of my book.

Young is concentrating on trying to explain why the triune nature of God is so important. What he writes here is the strongest denunciation of the evangelical faith yet to appear in his book.

He begins, again autobiographically, by rehearsing the steps that led to the writing of *The Shack*. He seems to reveal the supposed background to the novel to a greater degree than any other chapter.

Young grew up writing short stories, poems, and songs to get his "inside world out" (235).

1. He didn't feel whole enough to write *The Shack* until he turned fifty. He had reached a place of contentment. He did not write to impress or to serve an agenda, but he wrote as a gift for his children. He says he wanted "to say to them, 'Let me tell you about the God who actually showed up and healed my broken heart, not the god I grew up with in my modern evangelical Christian fundamentalism'" (236).

Yet this account of how *The Shack* came into being is incomplete in significant ways (see below).

2. He wrote conversations between himself and God about any topic that he thought would interest his kids. He eventually created a story with characters through whom he could represent his own story. Out of his own great losses, he wrote what he would want to say to his own children. He found that his own experience of God while growing up was "of little comfort. In fact, that God was considered the originator of evil, a distant deity who had a plan that included the torture of a child. One can't run to God if God is the perpetrator" (238).

3. Young states that to him God the Father was "a distant deity" and different in character from Jesus – "that God" was disappointed in Young, and Young felt betrayed. Young describes "that God" as a "one-alone God" who didn't show up at the shack. Young is speaking of Mack's experience as his own here. "In some scenarios," Young writes, "Jesus comes to protect us from that God's vengeance or just retribution. That God needs to be appeased, and failure is met by wrath and judgment" (238-239).

4. God must be triune, a Trinity, not a single God, in order for love and relationship to exist. In the three persons in One, there is the "great dance of face-to-face-to-face" relationship.

5. "Theirs is the mutual interpenetration of One with the Other without any diminishment or absorption of Person. This is the grand celebration of relationship in which all creation is created" (239).

6. "This is a God who is Love – a God who cannot be anything that is not Love" (239).

7. Young concludes by saying, "And frankly, I don't need a God who knows how to be alone. When I am in the middle of devastation and loss, I need a God who knows how to be *with*" (240). He needs the Papa of *The Shack*, "an all-consuming fire of relentless affection wrapped in the person of a large black

African woman. And She is not alone. With Her are Two, and the Three together are One" (240).

The Biblical Response

Young seems to feel the need to make one final scathing denunciation of the faith in which he grew up. What he says here makes it clear that Christianity, as he has known it, is unacceptable. It is no wonder that he and Kruger talk about forming a new movement, a reformation, and that Paul Young may be the new Martin Luther (as cited in the introduction, p. 8).

Let's note the severity of the distortion involved in the preceding summary:

(1) Young leaves out of his narrative important details that would help readers more clearly understand what he says about himself and what led to the writing of his novel for his kids. Sometime prior to 2004, Paul Young converted to universal reconciliation (UR). At our forum meeting in early 2004, he delivered his 103-page paper, asserting that he was giving up his "evangelical paradigm" and embracing UR. The following month at the forum, I read my paper opposing UR, but Young had stopped attending. Apparently, he then began writing the novel for his children. So Young leaves out of his story this conversion to UR.

Also, he does not reveal that his novel for his children was filled with UR. When he considered publishing it for adults, his two pastor friends didn't like the UR in it, so the three of them spent a year rewriting it. The extent to which the final product was the work of the combined efforts of three people later became the basis of a lawsuit in which the two pastors sued Paul Young over their part in the success of the novel. These details are available on a couple of websites.[26] Thus it is the second edition that people read as *The Shack*.

So this is the whole story of how *The Shack* was published and became a success. I think that this complete story would show many people that this novel is not just fiction, but it has a determined theological

---

26   Sarah Weinman, "The flak over 'The Shack,'" *Los Angeles Times,* July 13, 2010. *http://articles.latimes.com/2010/jul/13/entertainment/la-et-the-shack-20100713* (accessed June 6, 2017).

viewpoint that undermines Christian faith. Its success is due in part to the cover-up of its theological views. In his 2004 paper, he describes the place of "contentment" that he reached when he was fifty as his conversion to UR. For Young to say that he wrote his novel "with no agenda" appears to be disingenuous.[27]

In several points that I've listed above, Young slanders the God of the Bible and Jesus Christ. Note that in the first point he says that the God who healed him was not the "god" of evangelical Christianity. I would tend to agree, although I take exception both to his spelling of "god" with a little "g" and his *God* with a capital "G." The new "God" (which should be a little "g") is not the God of the Bible or Christian belief, as billions of Christians would attest from the time of the apostles until now. In my appendix on Athanasius, I give proof that it is Paul Young who is worshipping a different, foreign god.

The reality seems to be that the God of the Bible was trying to get Young's attention through much of his life. He faults God here for not showing up, but I suspect Young departed from God. The fault lies not with God but with Young, as his paper of 2004 makes clear. Having turned from God, Young discovered a deity more to his liking, one who is only love and not also holy and just. Young seems to have become uncomfortable with the God of the Bible.

Thus, Young forsakes the God belonging to "evangelical Christian fundamentalism." He throws God "under the bus" driven by the enemy of the cross, Satan himself!

How many of those now reading this book are willing to join with Paul Young in his rejection of the God of evangelical Christianity?

(2) He further slanders (blasphemes) the God of Christianity by describing him as the "originator of evil, a distant deity" whose "plan included the torture of a child." This child would be Jesus. Under *Lies*, chapters 17 and 19, I respond to this last idea that God acted as a "torturer" of Christ. How can a person who professes to have a deep relationship with God use such terminology? But it is nothing new. His paper of

---

27 So he claimed in his interview with Oprah Winfrey (dated July 9, 2017) as replayed on Young's website (wmpaulyoung.com/i-want-to-be-more-like-oprah-watch-interview) dated July 16, 2017.

2004 is filled with blasphemy of this sort. It reveals a heart dark with sin and under Satan's influence.

There is no way that God can be the author of evil. Jesus reveals who that author is – the devil. The Bible reveals Satan as such in Genesis 3, and Jesus confirms that Satan (the devil) is a murderer *from the beginning*, and that there *is no truth in him*. Satan *is the father of lies* (John 8:44). Satan is the *evil one* (John 17:15). And God is not distant: *God did this so that men would seek him and perhaps reach out for him and find him, though he is not far from each one of us. For in him we live and move and have our being* (Acts 17:27-28). He is so near that he became human to identify with us, and he has promised to be with his people to the end of this age (Matthew 28:18-20).

For Young to say that God "is the Perpetrator" (of evil, evidently) is unwarranted, evil speech. One wonders if Young would apply these words to all of his own so-called "broken experiences" that included his own sins. Did God perpetrate these if God is the "Perpetrator" of evil? Is this the way that Young seeks to ease the guilt of conscience – by blaming God? What of his own culpability?

With this kind of speech – slander – Young has become the instrument of evil. Even though Young would claim that he has some kind of relationship with God, this kind of speech shows that this claim is false. We may well ask, "Why, Paul Young, would you resort to this sort of blaspheming the God of the Bible? Does it not betray the fact that your embrace of UR does not lead you after all to being a 'more loving person,' as you claimed in 2004? If love is supreme for you, why is it not displayed toward all those Christians and evangelicals who you claim are worshipping the wrong God?"

(3) Young pits the God of wrath and judgment against Jesus, as found "in some scenarios." This is the old line of liberal theology, which is totally opposite to the witness of Jesus himself who reveals to us who God is (John 1:18 and chapters 14-17). He said that he and the Father are one – the same in essence (John 10:30; compare Hebrews 1:1-3). Jesus is not different in character from the Father. Since Young makes no attempt to separate himself from this scenario, he apparently agrees with it.[28] Yet how could this be true if in the eternity yet to come the Father and the Son enjoy equal prominence in the New Jerusalem? Both are its temple, both are its light, and both share the throne (Revelation 21:22-22:5). Thus, we discover another slander of the God of the Bible. The God of the Bible is triune, three-in-one, and each One fully and equally shares the divine nature. Believers are saved to enjoy a relationship with this One, who is not the god of UR.

In points 4 and 5 Young builds upon what he said earlier about the sexual nature of God (*Lies*, chapter 10). There is the "mutual interpenetration" among the Godhead. It is not clear, but Young seems to suggest that this interpenetration has sexual connotations for the nature and actions of the Triune God. Young should be required to address this issue. He remarks that all creation was created in this relationship.

Young is wrong to say that all creation, which includes all humanity, was created "in" God, but he repeats this elsewhere in *Lies* and in his novel *Eve* (see my discussion under *Lies*, chapters 3, 10, and 27).

I repeat what I earlier said: all creation was not created in God or in Jesus. Instead, creation is external to God. Otherwise, the result is a deified humanity and deified zebras, monkeys, and whatever! Only believers are identified as being *in Christ* or *in God* (by virtue of being in Christ) by being born again – having a spiritual birth (John 3). This rebirth does not make them little deities, but they are adoptees into God's family:

> *If you belong to Christ, then you are Abraham's seed, and heirs according to the promise.* (Galatians 3:29)

> *That we might receive adoption to sonship. . . . So you are no longer a slave, but a son; and since you are a son, God has made you also an heir.* (Galatians 4:5, 7)

> *The Spirit you received brought about your adoption to sonship. . . . Now if we are children, then we are heirs – heirs of God and co-heirs with Christ, if indeed we share in his sufferings in order*

---

28   Over several paragraphs he takes this position in his conversation with Stuart Hazeldine, the producer of the film, *The Shack*, under an article titled, "Does 'The Shack' Teach Universalism?" as found on Young's website, wpy@wmpaulyoung.com, dated 7-13-17.

that we may also share in his glory. (Romans 8:15, 17; note also verse 23)

(4) This point repeats the single most important doctrinal belief of UR: God is love. UR believes that this attribute limits God's other attributes. To say that God "cannot be anything that is not Love" is both true and not true. It is true that all the time and in every action God is love. But it is not the only character trait of God. God also is holy and just all the time and in every action, as well. To ignore this truth results in a truncated definition of God in his character and in his actions, which means that God ceases to be God – perfect in all his attributes. The god of UR is not truly God.

(5) I simply note that the evangelical faith rooted in the Bible and reaffirmed throughout the centuries is the source of our proper understanding of the triune nature of God and of the Christian's intimate relationship with him. Because Christians have placed their faith in Christ, they are in Christ, and because Christ is in the Father, they are in the Father, and he is in them. This intimacy with God is one of the great messages repeated in the Upper Room Discourse given just before Jesus went to the cross:

> *On that day you will realize that I am in my Father, and you are in me, and I am in you. . . . If anyone loves me, he will obey my teaching. My Father will love him, and we will come to him and make our home with him.* (John 14:20, 23)

> *That all of them may be one, Father, just as you are in me and I am in you. May they also be in us so that the world may believe that you have sent me. . . . I in them and you in me. May they be brought to complete unity to let the world know that you sent me and have loved them even as you have loved me. . . . I have made you known to them, and will continue to make you known in order that the love you have for me may be in them and that I myself may be in them.* (John 17:21, 23, 26)

Jesus prayed for this for his disciples and others – a unity with the Father. This relationship is the great privilege of every Christian, but not of those who deny the God and the Christ of the Bible, who spurn the required believing, the faith, that puts people into this intimate relationship. Jesus said this privilege comes to those *who believe in me through their* [the disciples'] *message* (John 17:20). Subsequently, Christians are to grow deeper in their relationship with God and mature, as the Apostle wrote of his own ministry: *We proclaim him, admonishing and teaching everyone with all wisdom, so that we may present everyone perfect in Christ* (Colossians 1:28).

The Apostle wrote that they should continue to grow until they come to the fullness of Christ:

> *We will in all things grow up into him who is the Head, that is, Christ. From him the whole body, joined and held together by every supporting ligament, grows and builds itself up in love, as each part does its work.* (Ephesians 4:15-16)

Young's "lie" of this chapter ("God is One Alone") is truly a lie. No Christian denies that God is a triune being. It is a straw man. But the extent to which Young goes in order to demolish this lie leads him to slander Jesus and the Father in the most evil of ways. In a very real sense, this is the most slanderous chapter in his book. If my review is on target, no Christian should identify himself/herself with the teachings of Paul Young.

PART THREE

THE SOVEREIGNTY OF GOD

Questions

Is God in control of all things? Does he have a plan that includes all things? Was the cross in God's plan? Is God a cosmic abuser of his Son?

> *Chapter 3: "God is in control."
>
> *Chapter 4: "God does not submit."
>
> **Chapter 17: "The cross was God's idea."
>
> Chapter 18: "That was just a coincidence."
>
> *Chapter 19: "God requires child sacrifice."

In these important chapters (note the use of asterisks), Paul Young delivers some strong denials of biblical truth regarding the Christian understanding of the rule – the sovereignty of God. God ends up being one who is not in control, one who is surprised by the cross, and one who is a cosmic child abuser if he planned Jesus's death on the cross. These chapters unveil just how far a universalist will go in denying the Bible and making God in the image of human beings. These chapters belong together since they deal with the big issue of God's sovereignty – his control over all that happens in the universe.

*CHAPTER 20

"GOD IS IN CONTROL"

(*Lies*, chapter 3)

Summary

The most alarming statements in this chapter assert that God is not in control of everything and does not have a plan for everyone. The cross was not in God's plan; God is an artist, not a planner. Thus, it is a "lie" to say that "God is in control." He is not in control, Young asserts.

In chapter 3 of *Lies*, Paul Young makes several points.

1. He seeks to show that God and the word *control* are not compatible. The mess of the world is not part of God's plan. Christians who believe otherwise believe in a "grim determinism which is fatalism" (37).

2. He suggests that Christians who believe that everything is in God's plan tend to make God the author of evil (38).

3. Some things are simply "wrong" and are not in God's plan.

4. The cross was evil and not part of God's plan. God takes the cross and transforms it. (This idea of the cross being man's idea, not God's, makes up Young's lie number 17 and is discussed more fully there.)

5. God does not have a plan for our lives, but he has a relationship that he invites us to join; then he submits to our choices. God respects our lives more than "the plan" (39).

6. God is an artist, not a planner, so he is not discontent when his plans don't work out (41).

7. God reigns by being who "God is: love and relationship" (41).

8. The idea of control is not part of God's vocabulary; rather, submission is (42). We invented the idea of control from our need to maintain the "myth of certainty." Young asserts, "There is no sense of control in the relationship among the Father, Son, and Holy Spirit" (42). We were created in the "same love and relationship" that exists in the Godhead (42). God "submits" to our choices and joins us in the "resulting mess of relationship" (43).

The Biblical Response

All of the foregoing points are either overstated or are contradicted by the Bible.

When Christians talk about God's plan, we simply mean this: God is omnipotent and omniscient – God is all powerful and able to accomplish anything that doesn't violate his character, such as sin; God is all-knowing, so nothing takes God by surprise. Thus, everything is in God's plan, but he does not author or originate everything in it. God did not originate evil, such as expressed by the rebellion of Satan and the fall of Adam and Eve, but God foreknew about evil and allowed it, because in the end it brings greater glory to God. He created human beings with a free will to choose to fall if they wish, so that in the end, many will choose to love God – the very one who provides the way for humanity to come back to him by way of the cross. He did not create people as automatons or robots who would always do his bidding but would have no free will to choose contrary to God. All of this is included in his plan. God did not determine the rise of evil. Rather, he determined the cross and all that is connected with it as the means to remedy that evil part of the plan that he allowed.

Thus, Young is at least partially incorrect or wrong in all the points above and totally wrong in points 1 through 4. There is partial truth in Young's other points regarding relationship, but not in the absolute way that he states them.

Regarding points 6 and 8, the Bible makes it clear that God is in control of everything. Chapters 40 to 46 of Isaiah speak of God's strength, power, and majesty. Then we read of his greatness, righteousness, and justice. Finally, he says to Isaiah, *My purpose will stand, and I will do all that I please* (Isaiah 46:10). In Daniel 4:35, even Nebuchadnezzar recognizes that God has the power to do as he pleases: *He does as he pleases with the powers of heaven and the peoples of the earth.* Romans 9:21 expresses the same concept: *Does not the potter* [representing God] *have the right to make out of the same lump of clay some pottery for noble purposes and some for common use?* Note also Acts 17:24-28.

Ephesians 1:3-14 also confirms God's plan and purpose. Note especially verse 11: God *predestined* [us] *according to the plan of him who works out everything in conformity with the purpose of his will.* Note the word *everything.* There are many other texts, too.

Young's words (in point 8) that God submits to us are true in the sense that God includes our sins and mistakes and choices in his plan, but he does not determine these. To assert that God and people equally submit to the other, however, is false. This belief arises from Young's determination in *The Shack* to build a case for a "pure relationship" between God and his children in which there is neither authority nor subordination expressed by any of the parties involved. More on this is in *Burning Down the Shack.*[29]

Point 4 above is especially pernicious. Contrary to what Young wrote, the cross was in God's plan and foreordained from before time, before God ever created anything. Note several texts:

This man [Jesus] *was handed over to you by God's set purpose and foreknowledge.* (Acts 2:23)

They did what your power and will had decided beforehand should happen. (Acts 4:28)

God presented him as a sacrifice of atonement. (Romans 3:25)

For he chose us in him before the creation of the world to be

---

29   James De Young, *Burning Down the Shack* (Washington, D.C.: WorldNetDaily, 2010) 122-124.

holy and blameless in his sight. In love he predestined us to be adopted as his sons through Jesus Christ. (Ephesians 1:4-5)

God made him who had no sin to be sin for us.
(2 Corinthians 5:21)

In addition to all of those references, Isaiah 53 prophesied the death of Christ hundreds of years before it came to pass.

Regarding point 5, God does have a plan, and it includes relationship with God, but there is no conflict between the two. He never has to submit to relationship instead of his plan. To suggest that God chooses relationship over his plan is blasphemy.

Regarding point 6 above, God is not ever discontent due to being an artist and needing to modify his plan. Rather, there is nothing in the universe outside of his plan. Thus, God is never discontented. Because God is omniscient, knowing all things for all times, there is never the need for a plan B. The very mention that somehow God's plans "don't work out" demonstrates a very small understanding of who God is. Again, Young seems to be molding God in Young's image, which is blasphemy.

Where would this limitation of God's knowledge be applied? To the way that the stars and the planets move? To the fall and rebellion of Satan against God in heaven? Did this take God by surprise? Was it not allowed in his masterful plan?

In Matthew 25:41, Jesus is dealing with those who either have or have not treated him well. The *cursed* will *depart into the eternal fire **prepared** for the devil and his angels* (author's emphasis). The blessed will take the inheritance *of the kingdom **prepared** for you since the creation of the world* (Matthew 25:34, author's emphasis). The form of the Greek word for *prepared* is in both places a perfect passive participle, meaning that both the destiny of the fire and the destiny of the kingdom were settled long ago and remain settled, at least from the creation onward. Jesus speaks from the future point of his coming as the Son of Man in his glory – an event still future to us. Thus, from the origin of hell for Satan and the events that brought his fall about to all the future events that encompass why the blessed have an expectation of entering Jesus's kingdom, including why Jesus came, what he did, and how believers responded, all are included in this "preparation." Thus, everything in the entire universe has been planned (prepared) at least for the time between the creation and the second coming of Christ. This period covers all that time covers. Nothing is outside this spectrum except God himself. Therefore, the event of the cross was foreseen and planned for from at least that far back. Also, it is biblical to claim that everything before creation and after Christ's return is also part of God's plan.

Here's an additional thought regarding God's omniscience and omnipotence. All that is good in God's foreknowledge, in his plan, he brings to pass by his power. That is, it is God who has not only planned all the good in the universe, including redemption by means of Jesus Christ, but he also brings it into existence.

Regarding point number 7, it is correct to say that God is love and relationship, but saying only this is misrepresentative. God is much more, including holy, just, righteous, good, and light. What Young has asserted is the classic expression of universalism: love is the supreme attribute of God and limits all his other attributes. But when one embarks down this road of limiting some of God's attributes, God is no longer God, and the Bible never supports such a limitation. The god of universal reconciliation is too small!

The way that Young describes God in this chapter means that God is surprised by things that he did not know about or plan for. He needs to adapt and change his plan. This violates the truth of God's omniscience and omnipotence. Young creates God according to Young's limited image and likeness. Young's god is not the all-sufficient, all-encompassing God of the Bible.

Can you imagine what happens when we extend to the whole universe the image Young imposes on God's character the way he does here? The implications are staggering!

Young has a similar passage in his novel *Eve*, where he denies that God has a settled plan or purpose.[30]

Young's "lie" here is exactly the truth of the Bible. God is in control of all things. Young, not Christians, is the one who lies.

---

30   Wm. Paul Young, *Eve* (New York: Howard Books, 2015), 181.

*CHAPTER 21

"GOD DOES NOT SUBMIT"

(*Lies*, chapter 4)

Summary

From the meaning of the Golden Rule, Young builds the idea of one of his great assertions flowing from his embrace of universal reconciliation (UR): mutual submission of human beings and God. We submit to God, and he submits to us. This reciprocity reflects what Young elsewhere identifies as the pure relationship that all people have with God. In this chapter, Young lays down concepts that he develops elsewhere in *Lies* (chapters 2, 10, 27).

Young begins this chapter as he frequently does – with a personal experience. I note the following points as the highlights of what he writes:

1. At a special conference, Young heard people of various religions discuss how the "spirit of Jesus" might cross all boundaries – ethnic, racial, and political (45).

2. From this starting point, Young asserts that all the religious books of the world appeal to what amounts to the Golden Rule: *Do to others what you would have them do to you* (Luke 6:31; also see Matthew 7:12).

3. At this point Young asks, "Do you think the Golden Rule applies to God?" (46). Young believes that it does – that God treats others "exactly" the way he wants to be treated. He reasons that this is so because so many religions have this basic rule. He

119

believes that the rule flows from the nature of God, which is love. "If God's nature is love then ours is, too, because we are created in the image of God" (46).

4. Young goes on: "Any command to love is to call us to *incarnate* the deepest truth of our being, love" (46). Young observes that he loves because he was first loved by God; he cites 1 John 4:19 here and adds, "And the way I know *how* to love others is by asking myself how I would want to be disciplined, or have boundaries" (46-47). This discussion of the Golden Rule leads Young to assert the main topic of the chapter.

5. A central aspect of this "other-centered love is the dynamic dance of mutual submission" (47). Submission originates in the "very being of God" (47).

6. "God is relational and therefore submits because God's nature is other-centered and self-giving love" (47).

7. "Submission has always been within the very being of the Triune God, person-to-person-to-person, face-to-face-to-face. Theirs is a divine dance of mutuality in which no Person is diminished or absorbed. It is true submission, in which the Other is known and respected" (47).

   Young admits that this idea that God is submissive may be difficult for some to accept or sound disparaging, "dragging our Holy God down to the level of human beings" (47).

8. But Young asserts that God does not intervene and keep us from making bad decisions. Instead, God submits to them and works through them. Love doesn't protect people from the results of their choices, but love also doesn't abandon people to them (48). As a corrective, Young adds that God's presence doesn't justify any "stupidity" on the part of people. He concludes: "God is opposed to anything that is not of Love's kind," yet he is "for us" in the midst of "the mess" (48).

9. Young suggests that "respectful" mutual submission is "where

authentic power and authority originate" (48). He asserts that the incarnation of God in Christ is "complete and utter submission to us," and the cross is where "God submits to our anger, rage, and wrath" (48). He also cites the example of Christ's washing the disciples' feet (49).

Young completes the chapter by citing the submission of his father to his mother in her frailty and illness and her submission to him. Such submission takes a lifetime to learn; it is better than power and control. It is a "call to be truly human" (49).

The Biblical Response

There is much here that could have been helpful, but because Young is rooted in UR, he distorts or omits biblical truth. Submission is a wonderful topic, but not as discussed by Young. As I pointed out above, further clarity comes to what Young is saying here by checking other chapters of *Lies*.

(1) How can the "spirit of Jesus" cross religious boundaries (a category Young doesn't name)? Is he saying something similar to what he has God assert in *The Shack* – that Jesus joins people on other roads to find them (182)? This is quite different from the exclusive claim that Jesus makes: *I am the way, and the truth, and the life. No one comes to the Father except through me* (John 14:6). And *I am the door; if anyone enters by me, he will be saved* (John 10:9 ESV). Jesus eliminates any claims that other religions may make that are opposed to his. Young here again expresses the tenets of universal reconciliation.

(2) Young's endorsement of a universal Golden Rule overlooks some obvious matters. Not all religions of the world are molded after founders or gods who are primarily motivated by love. Islam (where the idea of submission is supreme) and Hinduism come to mind. Further, observance of this rule is never given in the New Testament as the test of being a follower of Jesus (compare Matthew 7:12), of being in relationship with him, or as the sum of what it means to be a Christian. Rather, faith is what brings eternal life. It is surprising that Young would base

so much on performance, on doing, and on loving. Elsewhere, Young rejects performance and treats it as the opposite of relationship (see *Lies*, chapters 6 and 8). Young is terribly inconsistent here.

(3) Young's assertion that the Golden Rule applies to God is an error. To claim that God treats people "exactly" the way he wants to be treated is not true. While God desires his people to love him and to reciprocate the love Jesus has for us, God's love certainly exceeds that which his followers can reciprocate. *We love because he first loved us* (1 John 4:19). *Greater love has no one than this, that he lay down his life for his friends* (John 15:13). But in all kinds of ways, we are not able to reciprocate adequately. We cannot extend grace, forgiveness, gentleness, and a myriad of other things, as God does. We cannot love the world as God does (John 3:16). From another perspective, God rightly judges the world, but we are not judges of God. *He will judge the world in righteousness; he will govern the peoples with justice* (Psalm 9:8). *There is only one Lawgiver and Judge, the one who is able to save and destroy. But you – who are you to judge your neighbor?* (James 4:12).

In addition, while we have love as part of our nature because we are made in the image of God, this love has been greatly flawed because of the fall. For Christians, it is a love that comes from God because they are born again, and it becomes a reality by the work of the Spirit, as *fruit* from him (Galatians 5). Before conversion, Christians were enemies, in a state of hostility, and alienated from God. *Once you were alienated from God and were enemies in your minds because of your evil behavior* (Colossians 1:21). They were *dead in trespasses and sins* and *by nature deserving of wrath* (Ephesians 2:1, 3). That is the nature of people prior to regeneration and salvation. Young's assertion that love is the nature of all people overlooks these texts and the fall in Genesis 3. It is derived from UR, not from the Bible.

(4) Young's assertion that any command to love is a call to "incarnate the deepest truth of our being, love" is further developed in chapter 27 of *Lies*. Young defines sin (*hamartia*) as whatever "negates the truth of who people are" (229). Thus, Young's identification of love as the "truth of who people are" is consistent with how he defines sin, as the opposite of love. The only problem is that such definitions are wrong on both counts. Sin is much different than this; it violates God's law, nature, and glory. *For all have sinned and fall short of the glory of God* (Romans 3:23). And love is not the truth of who people are, because that premise overlooks the fall of Genesis 3. Only those who are regenerated, who have a new birth, have the capacity to love God and others as they should. But Young is consistent with his UR, which asserts that love is the supreme attribute of God.

For Young to assert in point 5 above that the central aspect of "other-centered love" is mutual submission and that submission originates in the "very being of God" is a distortion. There is no such idea in the Bible that God submits equally to humans. While Young tries to find mutual submission in the Triune God (point 7), he totally overlooks the fact that there is also a subordination of roles. The Father and Jesus sent the Holy Spirit; the Father sent the Son.

> *But if I do judge, my decisions are right, because I am not alone. I stand with the Father, who sent me. . . . The one who sent me is with me; he has not left me alone, for I always do what pleases him. . . . If God were your Father, you would love me, for I came from God and now am here. I have not come on my own; but he sent me.* (John 8:16, 29, 42)

> *This is love: not that we loved God, but that he loved us and sent his Son as an atoning sacrifice for our sins.* (1 John 4:10)

We know too that the Son delights to obey the Father: *But the world must learn that I love the Father and that I do exactly what my Father has commanded me* (John 14:31). In Hebrews 10:9, we read that Christ said, *Here I am, I have come to do your will.* These roles are never reversed as though the Father becomes subordinate to the Son and submits to him; so it is with the other roles.

Young also asserts that God's nature is "other-centered and self-giving love," but this is not the total truth. God is also righteous and holy – a jealous God who will not give his glory to another, nor will Jesus. *Do not worship any other god, for the LORD, whose name is Jealous, is a jealous*

God (Exodus 34:14). *I have given them the glory that you gave me, that they may be one as we are one. . . . I want those you have given me to be with me where I am, and to see my glory, the glory you have given me because you loved me before the creation of the world* (John 17:22, 24). God rightly demands to be glorified, and his creatures, especially the redeemed Christians, delight to glorify him. Note the benedictions in the epistles: *To the only wise God be glory forever through Jesus Christ* (Romans 16:27). *To the only God our Savior be glory, majesty, power, and authority, through Jesus Christ our Lord, before all ages, now and forevermore* (Jude 25). For Young to talk about mutual submission in which there is no authority nor subordination is slandering God.

Again, Young calls this mutual submission a "divine dance of mutuality in which no Person is diminished or absorbed." These words define *perichoresis* that he uses in describing the Godhead in chapter 10 of *Lies*, where he seeks to describe God as having a sexual nature and states that everyone is in relationship with him.

Young concludes that God is relational, as described in point 6, and that he submits to people, but God is much more. For example, he is the Judge of the whole world and will do what is right: *Will not God, the Judge of the whole world do right?* (Genesis 18:25). *I am not seeking glory for myself; but there is one who seeks it, and he is the judge* (John 8:50). *For we know him who said, "It is mine to avenge; I will repay," and again, "The Lord will judge his people"* (Hebrews 10:30). Jesus has been given the task of judging those who reject him. *But if I do judge, my decisions are right, because I am not alone. I stand with the Father, who sent me* (John 8:16). *For judgment I have come into this world, so that the blind will see and those who see will become blind* (John 9:39). To follow Young's reasoning, God is not transcendent, but only immanent (present). Such reasoning also finds expression in Young's assertion that God created everything, including human beings, "in him."

Christians are in relationship with God as Father and with Jesus Christ as Brother. The Lord's Prayer in Matthew begins by addressing God as our Father in heaven (Matthew 6:9). *Both the one who makes men holy and those who are made holy are of the same family. So Jesus is not ashamed to call them brothers* (Hebrews 2:11). Christians are to pursue a deeper relationship in knowing God, just as Paul expressed it. He wanted to *press on toward the goal to win the prize for which God has called me heavenward in Christ Jesus* (Philippians 3:14). Yet Jesus and the apostles show us that our relationship with the Godhead is not equally submissive. We still seek to do God's will; we do not ask him to do our will. It is not surprising that Jesus taught us to pray (in the "Lord's Prayer"): "Your kingdom come, your will be done . . ." (Matthew 6:10).

Young's concern that his remarks may be "disparaging our Holy God" is right on. This is exactly what he is doing in this chapter.

Regarding point 8, Young's concern that God's presence in mutual submission should not be used to justify any "stupidity" is a huge understatement. What about a perversion and distortion of the truth? What of heresy? Is not Young's propagation of UR something that is "not of love's kind"? There can hardly be a greater evil than the attempt to deceive God's people and lead them away from God and the Lord Jesus. The promise of UR that people can change their destiny after death is a huge deceit (*Lies*, chapter 21). Note what harsh words the Apostle Paul uses of those who propagate error, as he says: *let him be eternally condemned* (Galatians 1:8). All of Galatians 1 and 2 Corinthians 11 describe the Apostle's revulsion toward those who misled the people.

In the ninth point, Young somewhat inconsistently asserts that "authentic power and authority originate" in mutual submission. Elsewhere he excludes authority and subordination in a "circle of relationship" (*The Shack*, 122-124). I think it is extreme for Young to say that the incarnation is "complete and utter submission to us." The Bible says it is an act of humility, but Jesus submitted to the Father, not to us.

> *Who, being in very nature God, did not consider equality with God something to be grasped, but made himself nothing, taking the very nature of a servant, being made in human likeness. And being found in appearance as a man, he humbled himself and became obedient to death – even death on a cross.*
> (Philippians 2:6-8)

He did not "submit completely and utterly" to us in one area – he did not take on himself our sinful nature: *For we do not have a high priest who is unable to sympathize with our weaknesses, but we have one who has been tempted in every way, just as we are – yet was without sin* (Hebrews 4:15). It is absolutely possible to be fully human without having a sin nature – Adam and Eve were prior to the fall. It was absolutely necessary for Jesus to be without sin. But Young does not believe that people have a fallen, sinful nature.

More importantly, God did not submit to us at the cross, to "our anger, rage, and wrath." Rather, the cross was a demonstration of God's anger toward sin, where his wrath was satisfied. As cited earlier, Romans 3:21-26 and Isaiah 53 describe God's judgment on sin. Young distorts the meaning of the cross and makes the cross man's idea, not God's, and he also rejects penal substitution. (Young's distorted view of the cross occurs in chapters 17 and 19 of *Lies*.)

The great need was not that the anger of human beings had to be satisfied (which anger was illegitimate, anyway), but for God's anger to be satisfied, which was legitimate. *God presented him as a sacrifice of atonement, through faith in his blood* (Romans 3:25). Young has this backwards. Why? Because he submits the glory, the majesty, and the greatness of God to human restriction. He puts man – humanity – at the center, and does not put God at the center! His UR prevents God from being angry toward sin. Young's "lie" here, that "God does not submit," is the absolute truth in light of what he says in this chapter.

CHAPTER 22

"THE CROSS WAS GOD'S IDEA"

(*Lies*, chapter 17)

Summary

In short, what Young asserts here is that God did not plan for the cross – the death of Christ. God did not originate the cross (148-149). It was man's idea, but God submitted to the cross to destroy its power. If God did originate the cross, then God is a "cosmic abuser," a "cruel and monstrous god." This chapter is one of the most strategic and theologically evil in the entire book.

The primary question that Young asks is, "Who originated the Cross?" (148). Young is not reluctant to answer that God did not, and his explanation is so blasphemous that, for the record's sake, I quote it in full.

"If God did, then we worship a cosmic abuser, who in Divine Wisdom created a means to torture human beings in the most painful and abhorrent manner. Frankly, it is often this very cruel and monstrous god that the atheist refuses to acknowledge or grant credibility in any sense. And rightly so. Better no god at all, than this one" (149).

This is not the first time that Young has used such strong, slanderous language about the cross and the death of Christ. In his paper of 2004, he said that those who teach the doctrine of eternal torment make Jesus "a million times more vicious and vindictive" than Pharaoh, Nero, and Hitler put together.[31] Young said more. Because Jesus did not make an eternal payment to atone for sins, "Calvary was nothing but a farce, a

---

31   Wm. Paul Young, "Universal Reconciliation," 22.

burlesque, a travesty, and a sham. Jesus died a failure and in vain and never redeemed anyone from anything. . . . And if he is not the Savior of men, then he is not even a good man, but a liar, and therefore a rogue and a deceiving rascal. Salvation is a mere myth."[32]

Young makes similar slanderous statements in his other novels, *Cross Roads* and *Eve*. Reviews of these novels are on my website.[33]

These outrageous statements I'll answer below, after I cite the points that Young is making in this chapter:

1. God did not originate the cross, but people did in their "blind commitment to darkness" (149).

2. God submitted to our device of "brokenness" and destroyed its power.

3. God submitted to us both in Jesus's incarnation and before the creation of the world (Revelation 13:8). God knew that his "own children" would "attempt to kill Life" (150).

4. We "religious people" would interpret this sacrifice to mean that "it was God who killed Jesus, slaughtering Him as a necessary appeasement for His bloodthirsty need for justice" (150-151). Here Young cites the prophecy of Isaiah 53.

5. God "redeemed" our "evil" and "rescued it from its intent, thus becoming a statement of true justice" (152).

6. In the cross of Jesus, God was "submitting to our torture machine and transforming it" into an icon that we now hold dear. There is nothing so evil or broken that God "won't climb into it." The cross symbolizes "the God who is hope for us all" (153).

The Biblical Response

Let me address these points.

In discussing the "lie" of *Lies* in chapter 3 above, I cite several texts that affirm that the death of Christ was part of God's everlasting plan. God, not human beings, originated it. God purposed the death of Christ

---

32   Wm. Paul Young, "Universal Reconciliation," 29.

33   James De Young, *burningdowntheshackbook.com* (accessed June 12, 2017).

for a very deliberate reason that human beings never could have imagined. Fallen human beings would/could never have imagined the death of Jesus Christ on their behalf. Satan would have deceived them from doing so, for in the death of Christ, the second one of the Trinity, God initiated the action that will bring about both the destruction of death itself and the destruction of Satan, as cited in Hebrews 2:14-17 earlier. Neither mankind nor Satan ever would have created the idea of the death of Christ. God himself planned that he would join the human race, which would rebel against him; in this way he would provide the only way back to himself that humans could willingly choose.

In his novel *Eve*, Young makes a similar statement that the cross was not God's idea.[34]

In contrast to points 2 and 3 above, God did *not* submit to our device of the cross. Note that we are not talking about the device, the cross, per se, but what it stands for. The cross stands for the judgment of God against sin. That's why people did not originate the idea of the death of Christ, but God did. The cross was simply a very evil form of capital punishment that man created. But this is not the point. The death of Christ is the point, and humans did not originate the idea of his death.

It is no doubt because of Young's insistence in the previous chapter that God submits to humanity that he asserts here the idea that God submits to humanity's idea of originating the cross. Yet Young is completely wrong.

God originated the idea of the cross. If the death of Messiah is man's idea, why did the actual death of Christ seem so surprising to the Jewish apostles? Why did they protest the idea of his death? And if man created the idea, how is this reconciled with the fact that inspired men of the Old Testament era had already prophesied it as something that God would do? And who in the Old Testament era really grasped the idea that God himself would become a human being in order to become the sacrifice for sin?

Young is off target and mistaken in making the cross, rather than the death of Christ, the meaning and focus. But this is consistent with universalism that does not want to contemplate judgment. Young cannot

---

34   Paul Young, *Eve*, 237.

have God originate the idea of the cross, because that would mean that God originated the idea of the judgment associated with the cross. And universal reconciliation (UR) has no place for a God of judgment and justice, even though the Bible often speaks of God in this way. *How much more, then, will the blood of Christ, who through the eternal Spirit offered himself unblemished to God, cleanse our consciences from acts that lead to death, so that we may serve the living God!* (Hebrews 9:14). Recall the mention of judgment at the cross in Romans 3:25-26.

Note also that Paul Young almost always avoids the use of such theological terms as *sin* or *evil* in favor of terms emphasizing pure relationships, such as *blindness*, *brokenness*, and *darkness*. This represents the inherent rebellion found in universalism against anything that reflects the nature of God that would include justice and its expression in judgment and wrath.

Young's Omissions

What is especially glaring in points 1 to 3 is what Young does not say. He does not give the Bible's interpretation for what the death of Christ means. Because his focus reinterprets the cross as man's creation or origination, he rejects the cross as the place where God judges the weight of all humanity's sin as something that demanded an eternal sacrifice; *for the wages of sin is death* – eternal death. Every human being should have to make an eternal sacrifice for his personal sin, because the stain caused by sin can never be removed nor its accompanying guilt ever be alleviated. But Jesus Christ, as the God-man, could and did make *one sacrifice once for all for all time, obtaining eternal redemption*, as Hebrews repeatedly proclaims (9:12, 26-28; 10:9-10, 12-14, 18). This is the biblical idea of universalism! Note the extent of these verses.

In his paper of 2004, Young attacked evangelical teaching about eternal punishment for sin and claimed that because Jesus did not suffer eternally on the cross, he didn't obtain salvation. But Young is wrong. He repudiates these verses from Hebrews that say just the opposite. Jesus did die a death that had eternal consequences. Jesus paid the full price that God demanded as an *atonement*, a sacrifice, to pay for all the evil in the universe. *Christ died for sins, once for all, the righteous for the unrighteous, to bring you to God* (1 Peter 3:18).

Young's obsession with limiting the attributes of God to that of the love of God and relationship has blinded him from the true meaning of the death of Christ. The cross is not about our blindness, but it is about God's justice and the enormity of our sin. Only when we believe is blindness removed.

Elsewhere in *Lies* Young says that the story of the blind man being healed is his favorite. He should read it again, for it speaks of physical and spiritual blindness. Jesus said that faith was necessary to be able to see spiritually (John 9:35-38). Jesus added, *For judgment I have come into the world, so that the blind will see and those who see will become blind* (verse 39). For those, like the Pharisees, who were spiritually blind, Jesus said, *If you were* [physically] *blind, you would not be guilty of sin; but now that you claim that you can see* [spiritually], *your guilt remains* (verse 41).

As all other people who confess UR, Paul Young has decided to join the Pharisees. Note how this blindness to the reality of sin for those who don't believe in Jesus differs from Young's assertion that all people are blind to the reality of their already being children of God.

So in light of what I've just written, we realize that with point 4, Young clearly becomes blasphemous. It is not we "religious people" who have "interpreted" Christ's death to mean that it was "God who killed Jesus, slaughtering Him as a necessary appeasement for His bloodthirsty need for justice." Young accurately cites Isaiah 53, which says several times over that God initiated the death of Christ to provide the basis for our forgiveness.

> *Surely he took up our infirmities and carried our sorrows,*
> *yet we considered him stricken by God, smitten by him and*
> *afflicted. But he was pierced for our transgressions, he was*
> *crushed for our iniquities; the punishment that brought us*
> *peace was upon him, and by his wounds we are healed. We*
> *all, like sheep, have gone astray, each of us has turned to his*
> *own way; and the LORD has laid on him the iniquity of us*
> *all. He was oppressed and afflicted, yet he did not open his*

mouth; he was led like a lamb to the slaughter, and as a sheep before her shearers is silent, so he did not open his mouth. By oppression and judgment he was taken away. And who can speak of his descendants? For he was cut off from the land of the living; for the transgression of my people he was stricken. (Isaiah 53:4-8)

Yet it was the LORD's will to crush him and cause him to suffer, and though the LORD makes his life a guilt offering, he will see his offspring and prolong his days, and the will of the LORD will prosper in his hand. After the suffering of his soul, he will see the light of life and be satisfied; by his knowledge my righteous servant will justify many, and he will bear their iniquities. Therefore I will give him a portion among the great, and he will divide the spoils with the strong, because he poured out his life unto death, and was numbered with the transgressors. For he bore the sin of many, and made intercession for the transgressors. (Isaiah 53:10-12)

But Young apparently believes that Isaiah is in error. He fails to do justice to this text and accept it as the divine interpretation of the death of Christ. This text is parallel to that of Romans 3:23-26. Jesus and the apostles cite Isaiah 53 as prophesying about Jesus Christ:

This was to fulfill what was spoken through the prophet Isaiah: "He took up our infirmities and carried our diseases." (Matthew 8:17)

It is written: "And he was numbered with the transgressors"; and I tell you that this must be fulfilled in me. Yes, what is written about me is reaching its fulfillment." (Luke 22:37)

This was to fulfill the word of Isaiah the prophet: "Lord, who has believed our message and to whom has the arm of the Lord been revealed?" (John 12:38)

The eunuch was reading this passage of Scripture: "He was led like a sheep to the slaughter, and as a lamb before the shearer is silent, so he did not open his mouth. In his humiliation he

was deprived of justice. Who can speak of his descendants?
For his life was taken from the earth." (Acts 8:32-33)

Romans 10:16 and 1 Peter 2:22 also refer to this chapter in Isaiah. So, not only did God prophesy of the death of Christ on the cross, but the New Testament writers also refer to Isaiah when they are explaining the salvation that God had planned.

Both in public appearances and in his novels, Young rejects the doctrine of penal substitution. This doctrine teaches that Jesus bore the penalty that our sins demanded to be paid, and he did it in our (the sinners') place. Thus, Jesus bore the penalty that I should have had to pay but was unable to pay.

Note the blasphemy in Young's statement. First, he says that this is how we humans "interpreted" the death of Christ. Apparently he is taking this idea from the translation *we considered him stricken by God.* Yet *considered* does not mean "interpreted" here. Rather, it has the sense of "esteemed," as in the English Standard Version or the King James Version, or "regarded," "reckoned," or to "give judgment of." The context makes it clear that a subjective interpretation is not involved, but that our estimation is that derived from God. It is God's evaluation of the death of Christ for others. For Young to reject God's estimation of Christ's death and to substitute his own is blasphemous.

Second, here is where Young asserts that if we believe that God brought about the death of Christ to pay for the eternal weight of human sin, then we make God a "cosmic abuser" of children (see *Lies*, chapter 19). But this is exactly what Isaiah 53 and many other texts assert. For Young to interpret this to mean that God is a cosmic abuser is to slander the God of the universe. For Young and others to speak such blasphemy makes them deserving of everlasting judgment. Thus, Young is greatly misinformed and misleading and lost.

Other points from Young's statement are blasphemous. He uses the words, "necessary appeasement for His bloodthirsty need for justice." First, appeasement is not the biblical idea behind *hilasmos*, which is better translated as "propitiation" or "satisfaction," rather than "appeasement." The word *appeasement* is the way liberal theologians and universalists interpret the death of Christ. It means that some human devotee of a deity brings an offering to allay or appease the capricious anger of a deity.

But *satisfaction* indicates a payment made to satisfy what is justly required. It is an act of justice. It is the exact word used for the mercy seat over the ark of the covenant in the holy of holies as described in the Old Testament, particularly in Leviticus. On this solid plate of gold, the high priest once a year on the Day of Atonement (*yom kippur*) sprinkled the blood of a goat and a bull to "cover" the sins of the priests and of the people for the past year. Thus, on the Passover, Jesus shed his blood to accomplish eternal redemption so that sins could be forever forgiven, not just covered. These great truths are affirmed in Hebrews chapters 9 and 10 (cited above, especially 9:11-12 and 10:1-4) and Romans 3. The word *hilasmos* is used twice (Romans 3:26; 1 John 2:2) to describe Jesus Christ and his death on the cross. He is the propitiation or satisfaction or atoning sacrifice for our sins. First John 2:2 says that *He is the atoning sacrifice for our sins, and not only for ours but also for the sins of the whole world.*

For Young to use the words, "bloodthirsty need for justice" is slander of the worst kind. Young is making God the Father like the pagan deities of the Old Testament and those of the Greek and Roman world who often required child and human sacrifices to appease their ongoing appetites and capricious (unpredictable) demands. Paul Young is denying to the God of the universe, the one and only true God, the glory due to him alone. He blasphemes again.

The death of Jesus Christ was the satisfaction that God's justice required to pay for the sin and guilt – the consequences of which had never been satisfied before (Hebrews 10:4). Note the following verses:

Christ Jesus, whom God put forward as a propitiation [atoning sacrifice; the *hilasmos*] *by his blood, to be received by faith. This was to show God's righteousness, because in his divine forbearance he had passed over former sins. It was to show his righteousness at the present time, so that he might be just and the justifier of the one who has faith in Jesus.* (Romans 3:24-26 ESV). These last words point both to God's nature and to his actions.

In the fifth point above, Young misplaces the emphasis and distorts what is true. It is not that God is "redeeming" evil, which is standard universalism and found in his novels; rather, by the substitutionary death of Christ, God is redeeming people, purchasing people from enslavement to evil and setting them free. First Corinthians 6:20 tells us *you were bought at a price,* and Colossians 1:13 says, *For he has rescued us from the dominion of darkness and brought us into the kingdom of the Son he loves.* God is destroying evil and will bring it to an end in the future. Young's "true justice" is fake. The true justice is what the above cited texts say: God satisfied the justice that his nature as good and holy and righteous demanded, so that those who believe go free; they are released from the penalty and power of sin. No pagan deity was ever able to release its devotees this way. In the Bible, God initiates the action of redemption; he does not respond to some gift from a devotee.

In the sixth point, Young is again wrong when he says the cross symbolizes God submitting to us. Rather, the cross symbolizes God's judgment that required Christ's substitutionary death as payment for our sins. The cross does not symbolize "the God who is hope for us all" (153). It symbolizes deliverance from the penalty and power of sin that comes to those who believe; note the reference to faith in the quote from Romans 3. God is not the "hope for us all," but only for those who believe. Because of what Jesus did on the cross, we don't just have hope, but we have assurance of forgiveness and eternal life.

The idea of hoping for the salvation of all and for escape from hell's judgment is the regular expression of universalism. God never expresses such hope, and we slander God when we say we have such a hope and reject the way of salvation that God has provided in the death of Christ.[35] It is actually supreme rebellion for the creature to assert a hope that the Creator does not assert, but reveals just the opposite – that after death there is an everlasting destiny that cannot be altered (Hebrews 7:25).

Lies, chapters 3 and 17 go to the heart of what universalism's attack on Christian faith is all about. It is focused on the meaning of the cross of Christ as though it wasn't part of God's plan.

---

35   Young continues to repeat this hope on websites and in interviews. See Appendix 1 where in my fifth point I respond to Young's "hope" expressed on C. Baxter Kruger's website. He also repeats it on his website, wpy@wmpaulyoung.com in the article, "Does 'The Shack' Teach Universalism?" where Stuart Hazeldine interviews Young (dated July 13, 2017).

For Young to propose that the "lie" of this chapter ("The cross was God's idea") is a lie is itself a lie. The truth is that the cross was God's idea. It certainly wasn't man's idea, as witnessed by the statements that Young makes here.

The great hymn, "At Calvary," in its fourth stanza, had it right: "O the love that drew salvation's plan! O the grace that bro't it down to man! O the mighty gulf that God did span at Calvary."

CHAPTER 23

"THAT WAS JUST A COINCIDENCE"

(*Lies*, chapter 18)

Summary

In chapter 18 of his book, Young deals with the idea of coincidence – that all things happen by chance or randomly. Young asserts that there is purpose and that God is present in all that happens. This chapter seems to contradict what he says in previous chapters.

In this chapter he explains his special insight into the events that seem to be random. He begins by talking about children's language. He says that children speak the language of God – full of delight, amazement, and surprise. Young's exhortation is that adults need to return to their childlikeness to see the wonders of the world around them, which he equates with the kingdom of God. He says that God has "never lost the ability to speak 'children'" (156).

In somewhat of an aside, Young quotes G. K. Chesterton in his praise of children and their desire for things to be "repeated and unchanged." Chesterton suggests that God has the "eternal appetite of infancy" (157). It is not readily apparent why Young cites Chesterton. It's probably just to defend his statements about the wonderment that children have.

Moving toward his intended topic, Young says that "childhood was God's idea" and that children's language of simple trust and delight involves "the unexplainable and coincidence." Meaning is found by melding together disparate elements into "a new surprise" (157). He notes that God is an "expert at language," and that God created the whole world "by a single Word." Yet God comes to us and speaks our language – all of our "unique" languages (158).

Coincidence is "firmly a part of the language of a child" (158). It is also involved in the way God speaks to adults – by speaking to the child in them. God is "involved in the details of our lives" (159). There "are no chance encounters" and no true detours. People need to pay attention to their "part of participation with the flow of the redeeming genius and creativity of the Spirit . . . even in the midst of profound loss and agony" (159). With these last words, Young is giving an additional answer to the questions he raised earlier regarding the existence of suffering and evil in the world (*Lies*, chapter 16).

By citing an experience, Young illustrates that there are no coincidences. On a book-signing trip to South Africa, he read a portion from *Eve* that coincided with the experiences of several girls who were thinking of suicide. While Young thought that he had chosen the text on a whim or by chance, at "random and exempt from purpose," this experience convinced him that "nothing is apart from the abiding presence and activity of God" (163). Young concludes with his mantra (as he calls it): "Coincidence has a Name."

The Biblical Response

While this chapter has several things about language to commend, several other things are lacking on the topic of coincidence.

(1) The simplicity and humility of the mind of children is commended in Scripture by Jesus himself. Their simple faith or implicit trust should characterize adults who would want to enter the kingdom of God.

> *Jesus said, "I praise you, Father, Lord of heaven and earth, because you have hidden these things from the wise and learned, and revealed them to little children." (Matthew 11:25)*

> *He called a little child and had him stand among them. And he said: "I tell you the truth, unless you change and become like little children, you will never enter the kingdom of heaven.*

Therefore, whoever humbles himself like this child is the greatest in the kingdom of heaven." (Matthew 18:2-4)

Jesus said, "Let the little children come to me, and do not hinder them, for the kingdom of heaven belongs to such as these." (Matthew 19:14)

(2) It is commendable for Young to acknowledge that everything is according to a "purpose" and in the "presence and activity of God" and the Spirit, but notice his words. He does not use terms such as the "plan of God" or that God "originates" all things. Such language would put Young in contradiction with himself and his statements elsewhere. In chapter 3 of his book, he says that not everything is in God's plan, even some good or indifferent things. In chapter 4, he asserts that God submits to the plans of people. In chapter 17, he says that the cross was not in God's plan but came from man, and in chapter 19, he says that the idea of the sacrifice of Christ on the cross did not originate with God, but with man.

Either Young is in contradiction with these other chapters, or he does not fully or really believe that everything is in God's plan and is foreseen by God. He does not accept that God is omnipotent and omniscient in all things, as we can see in his third chapter. For Young to use language that affirms the "creativity of the Spirit," that all things occur according to a "purpose" and in the "presence and activity of God," allows for a syncretism (merging) of divine and human activity. In Young's concept of a pure relationship involving God and people, in which there is no authority and no submission of either party, God and people "give and take."

Finally, I believe that his understanding of "no coincidences" is truncated or revised to mean that there are coincidences, and things are left to chance or to a whim, because they are ultimately decided by a confluence of both the divine and human wills. In Young's understanding, this may mean that all things are not coincidences. In light of his commitment to universal reconciliation (UR) – that God in love submits to human beings and that all people have the divine nature within – God and people jointly determine all things. By this view there is nothing left to chance.

Yet, if there is here a syncretism or meshing of wills, then how does one decide whose will is the active or predominant one at a given time? In many cases, this knowledge is critical. Further, what happens when different people insist that their ideas are the correct ones? Without God's will being supreme, all sorts of evil could be justified.

(3) One other thing needs saying. Young encourages people to pay attention to what God may be saying to them in their "unique languages" and in their "coincidences," but what about listening to God speaking in the Bible? This idea is totally missing in this chapter and elsewhere. The Bible is inspired-by-God speech and is certainly fully authoritative to all Christians, but not to those who embrace UR.

The "lie" of chapter 18 is just that. No biblically informed Christian would say that things are "just coincidences." This is another straw-man argument.

CHAPTER 24

"GOD REQUIRES CHILD SACRIFICE"

(*Lies*, chapter 19)

Summary

In chapter 19, Young continues the ideas he introduced in chapter 17. He takes up the specific topic of the sacrifice of Christ on the cross and equates it with the idea that God's anger had to be appeased. He denies that "child sacrifice" is a biblical pattern.

Continuing what he began in chapter 17, Young asserts here that Christians believe that God requires a child sacrifice. On the surface, this is a straw man, since no Christian believes that God wants us to sacrifice our own children or the children of others to appease him.

But Young wants to take this further. He starts by recounting how many cultures around the world sacrifice their children to appease their gods. He goes on to bring in the idea that missionaries often sacrifice their children on the "altar of spreading the good news" about Jesus Christ. He faults Christian missions for often promoting this idea respecting children (167). Strangely, he talks about bed-wetting as one of the costs of being "a living sacrifice" (these words are apparently an allusion to Romans 12:1-2). He talks about the terrible practice in Uganda of sacrificing children to "territorial spirits."

I perceive that these are the points that Young seeks to make:

1. People seek justification for sacrificing children, actually or metaphorically, for whatever reason, by believing that God requires the sacrifice of children.

2. Brutal beliefs in parts of the world support the sacrifice of children for protection against evil spirits and financial ruin. According to the evangelical doctrine about sin, God required "the ultimate child sacrifice" – Jesus – to appease a sense of "righteous indignation and the fury of holiness."

3. Religion or nationalism or patriotism "wields power to justify its actions by grounding them in the purposes and will of God" (169). The Scriptures are used for the "perpetuation of horrendous abuse" (170).

4. The Old Testament clearly declares that God hates child sacrifice.

5. When Abraham attempted to offer up Isaac as a sacrifice, God was submitting to Abraham's choice to do so.

6. The story of Abraham and Isaac is not a story of God requiring child sacrifice, but rather "the opposite" (171). When God provided the ram as a substitute for Isaac, he showed that he did not require child sacrifice.

7. If the human race requires a sacrifice, "God will provide Himself" (171).

The Biblical Response

What is this chapter all about? It is not difficult to see that Young is laying the foundation for the belief that the cross was not God's idea, as I've discussed above regarding Young's chapter 17.

But there are additional fallacies here. Young's reflections on growing up on the mission field seem to betray an anger toward his past. My response to the points above is as follows:

(1) I believe that this point is overstated. While it may be true in some cases that children are harmed, not many justify this by linking it to the event of the cross.

(2) To link the event of the cross to how other deities are appeased in pagan cultures has serious problems.

First, Jesus was not a child who involuntarily died on the cross. He was an adult and willingly chose to become our atoning sacrifice for sin, as we read in Hebrews 10, which quotes Psalm 40. He was fully aware of the meaning of his impending crucifixion; Gethsemane makes this clear.

Second, Jesus went to the cross to deal with sin once for all – not to make the ground fertile, to end a drought, or to have offspring, as the pagans tried to accomplish with their sacrifices.

Third, Jesus arose from the grave to prove that his work was finished and accepted by the Father. No pagan deity ever became incarnate, died, and rose to be alive forevermore.

Fourth, Jesus died as the God-man, not as a human only. As God, his death has everlasting consequences. As human, he actually died.

Fifth, God was not appeased, but propitiated (I noted the difference when discussing Young's chapter 17). Payment had been made to satisfy justice, not caprice or whim.

Sixth, Jesus became the substitute for all people everywhere, as he provided the atonement – the removing of the penalty for sin. His death has universal significance. No pagan deity's sacrifice could have this power.

Seventh, the Old Testament's condemnation of child sacrifice inherently means that Jesus's death is not to be regarded this way. This observation deals with point 4 above.

There are many more reasons why making Jesus's death similar to the sacrifices demanded by pagan deities is blasphemous.

(3) This point falls under similar criticism as point 2. While the world's religions may seek such justification, the God who discloses himself in the record of the Bible is unique and commands allegiance from all peoples everywhere. The proof of Christianity being the only true religion, if we may call it a religion, is the resurrection of Jesus Christ and his return to heaven. He is alive today. This message of Easter still draws millions to Christ every day. He is coming again, as he states in John 14:2-3: *I am going there to prepare a place for you. And if I go and prepare a place for you, I will come back and take you to be with me that you also may be where I am.*

(4-7) Points 4 to 7 all concern the (almost) sacrifice of Isaac. Young is in error in what he says, because the Old Testament record tells us that God commanded Abraham to offer up Isaac. It was a test of Abraham's faith and obedience. This is what the authoritative interpretation given in Genesis 22 and Hebrews 11 affirms:

> By faith Abraham, when called to go to a place he would later receive as his inheritance, obeyed and went, even though he did not know where he was going. . . . By faith Abraham, even though he was past age – and Sarah herself was barren – was enabled to become a father because he considered him faithful who had made the promise. . . . By faith Abraham, when God tested him, offered Isaac as a sacrifice. He who had received the promises was about to sacrifice his one and only son, even though God had said to him, "It is through Isaac that your offspring will be reckoned. Abraham reasoned that God could raise the dead, and figuratively speaking, he did receive Isaac back from death. (Hebrews 11:8, 11, 17-19)

It was not an act to appease an angry deity; the text says nothing of this. For Young to read this into the text is an unfounded, evil interpretation. Further, the New Testament says that because Isaac was Abraham's *only son* (Genesis 22:2, 12, 16), Abraham's act was based in the belief that God would resurrect Isaac from the dead in order to keep the covenant that God had made regarding an offspring who would bring blessing to all the world.

> I will make you into a great nation and I will bless you; I will make your name great, and you will be a blessing. I will bless those who bless you, and whoever curses you I will curse; and all peoples on earth will be blessed through you. (Genesis 12:2-3)

In the events of Genesis 22, Abraham and Isaac thus typify God and Jesus Christ – both in the death of Christ on the cross and in his resurrection!

It is amazing how universalism has led Paul Young to distort so much of the biblical record regarding the sovereignty of God. Universal reconciliation (UR) asserts that God is a God of love and that love limits his other attributes. With this presupposition, Abraham's act simply cannot be an act commanded by God; it cannot typify the judgment of sin that God accomplished on the cross to deal with people's sin and sins. Thus, Young forces the Bible to agree with the basic assertions of UR. But if UR can distort the Bible this way, why can't the cults like Jehovah's Witnesses and major religions like Islam also do so?

The "lie" of this chapter is the truth if by "child sacrifice" we mean the death of Jesus Christ for sin. God did require his sacrifice, but Young takes the "lie" to describe the involuntary, torturous sacrifice of a child to appease a capricious deity. Taking it this way, the "lie" is false, morally evil, and a straw man.

Consider the precious words from stanza three of "How Great Thou Art":

> And when I think that God,
>   His Son not sparing,
> Sent Him to die,
>   I scarce can take it in –
> That on the cross, my burden
>   gladly bearing, He bled and died
> to take away my sin.

PART FOUR

SOTERIOLOGY: THE STUDY OF SALVATION

Questions

What does salvation mean? Is everyone already saved? Is anyone lost? What is hell? Does hell bring separation from God? Can people choose God after dying? What does sin mean? Does sin bring separation from God?

*Chapter 13: "You need to get saved."

*Chapter 15: "Hell is separation from God."

*Chapter 21: "Death is more powerful than God."

*Chapter 27: "Sin separates us from God."

In this final, fourth section, I bring together those chapters that deal with how people are saved, whether they are saved, and why they need to be saved. These chapters also clarify how a universalist understands salvation if no one is lost. Again, the asterisks indicate that all these chapters are crucial for understanding the heretical nature of UR and Paul Young's beliefs.

CHAPTER 25

"YOU NEED TO GET SAVED"

(*Lies*, chapter 13)

Summary

Universal reconciliation (UR) asserts that people do not have to come to Christ, accept him as Savior, and become saved. All people are already saved. Paul Young *confesses without reservation* that he believes in universal reconciliation.

In many respects this chapter is the high point of Paul Young's book, for in it he unveils in clear-cut language that he has embraced that heresy of which many have suspected and accused him. He unabashedly confesses his conversion to UR (118). For thirteen years I've been speaking and writing that Young is a universalist. Many doubted this. Others did not care. Now his words are clear, and every Christian should care.

Young opens the chapter by asserting that Christianity is often like making a sales pitch when marketing wares of various kinds. After "saying the sinner's prayer," new converts are expected to perform various tasks. Failure to follow through may put one in danger of "being eternally tormented in a lake of fire" (116-117).

Young asks how anyone could consider this to be "great news." He notes that because of this preaching, multitudes are abandoning the church. His remedy is to redefine who is a Christian. Here is my construction of the many points he makes.

1. To answer the questions of what the good news is and what the gospel is, Young answers that it "is *not* that Jesus has opened up

the possibility of salvation, and you have been invited to receive Jesus into your life" (117). He says the gospel is that "Jesus has already included you into His life, into His relationship" with God and with the Holy Spirit.

2. The good news is that Jesus did this without a person's vote and without his/her belief.

3. A person is saved either by what God did in Jesus or by what people do themselves. Obviously, people cannot save themselves.

4. "Saving faith is not our faith, but the faith of Jesus" (118).

5. God does not wait for our choice and then save us. Instead, God has "acted decisively and universally for all humanity. Now our daily choice is to either grow and participate in that reality or continue to live in the blindness of our own independence" (118).

6. At this point Young proclaims with absolute clarity what all this means. He writes, "Are you suggesting that everyone is saved? That you believe in universal salvation? That is exactly what I am saying! This is real good news!" (118).

7. This "has been blowing people's minds for centuries now" (118). This is Young's appeal to history.

8. He boldly proclaims, "Here's the truth" (119). With these words, Young cites the support for his claim that everyone is already saved. Everyone ever conceived was included in the death, resurrection, and ascension of Christ. He cites several passages and misinterprets them. He uses John 12:32 to say that God "dragged" all humanity to himself. He claims 1 Timothy 4:10 means that Jesus is the Savior of all, especially believers. He continues by saying that 1 John 1:3 indicates that every human being is in Christ, and that John 14:20 tells us that Christ is in all and Christ is in the Father. Then he says that 2 Corinthians 5 proves that when Christ died and rose, all people died and rose in him. Young notes that in an appendix he cites many texts that support these points.

9. Young enumerates three dimensions of the context of salvation (119). First, prior to the creation, all people were included; all were saved in eternity. He uses 2 Timothy 1:9 to attempt to support this. Second, using 2 Corinthians 5:19, he says that all people were included in the "birth, life, death, resurrection, and ascension of Jesus." Third, within the context of people's own present experience, people actively "participate to *work out* what God has *worked in*," and he cites Philippians 2:12-13 to support this. Young says our participation is essential.

10. We don't judge anyone by how he or she is stuck, broken, or lost, according to 2 Corinthians 5:16. We see everyone as one whom the Holy Spirit finds and celebrates. Young adds that we "don't offer anyone what has already been given; we simply celebrate the Good News with each one. *We have all been included*" (120, italics his).

11. Finally, Young adds that we don't participate in our salvation "in order to make it true; we do so because it is true" (121).

The Biblical Response

As shown above, this chapter is one of Young's more lengthy defenses of his theology, but it is almost all unbiblical. Many of his points are repetitious and flow from the one great center – universal reconciliation (UR). His confession of this is clear and unmistakable. No longer should anyone doubt what I (and others) have been saying since 2004: UR is embedded in *The Shack* and in Young's other novels. Many of the points that I've listed above can be dealt with together.

So what is the biblical evidence that contradicts the UR that Young presents here? His basic premise is that all humanity was created *in* God in Genesis 1 and 2 and that this means all people *have* the divine nature. It is the divine image in all humanity (73, 95). Thus, as God is good, so are all people. They are not "lost in sin."

But Young is wrong here. The Bible says that we are created in the "image and likeness" of God. We do not have the divine nature within us; we are not made divine (as I also argued when discussing *Lies*, chapter 10).

Further, Young never mentions the fall of humanity into sin as recorded in Genesis 3 and taken up in Romans 5:17 when the Apostle Paul says *by the trespass of the one man, death reigned through that one man.* Also 1 Corinthians 15:22 says that *as in Adam all die, so in Christ all will be made alive.* All humanity died in Adam, and only in Christ can all be made alive. But becoming alive in Christ is a matter of choice. The end of Romans 5:17 reads, *how much more will those who receive God's abundant provision of grace and of the gift of righteousness reign in life through the one man, Jesus Christ.* People must receive someone or something to be in Christ. Many texts show that no one is in Christ until that person accepts him as Savior and Lord. *He came to that which was his own, but his own did not receive him. Yet to all who received him, to those who believed in his name, he gave the right to become children of God – children born not of natural descent, nor of human decision or a husband's will, but born of God* (John 1:11-13). This involves confessing Christ by faith in order to be saved, as Romans 10:9-10 teaches (cited earlier).

Those who are in Christ are those who have accepted Christ by faith; the rest of humanity is not in Christ, contrary to what Young says in this chapter (note my earlier discussion of Ephesians 2-3). Only Christians are identified with Christ; that is, they are identified in him, in his death, resurrection, and ascension (but not in his birth, contrary to Young). The Apostle Paul says the believers at Colossae had been reconciled to God by believing. Until then they were enemies and hostile toward God. The Apostle identifies these believers as the only ones united in Christ:

> *Once you were alienated from God and were enemies in your minds because of your evil behavior. But now he has reconciled you by Christ's physical body through death to present you holy in his sight, without blemish and free from accusation, if you continue in your faith.* (Colossians 1:21-22)

> *Since, then, you have been raised with Christ, set your hearts on things above, where Christ is seated at the right hand of*

God. Set your minds on things above, not on earthly things.
For you died, and your life is now hidden with Christ in God.
(Colossians 3:1-3)

For in Christ all the fullness of the Deity lives in bodily form,
and you have been given fullness in Christ, who is the head
over every power and authority. (Colossians 2:9-10)

No texts affirm that all humanity is in Christ. Young has created this belief because of his UR, in spite of what the Bible says.

All that I've written thus far contradicts the claims that Young makes in points 1 through 5 above. Regarding number 4, it is a person's faith, not Christ's faith, that saves. After all, what is it that Jesus believed that could save people for their failure to believe? And Jesus did not exercise any faith in order to be saved, since he did not have a sin nature that would require him to be saved. Instead, he is the one who saves others, as Mary was told at the virgin conception of Jesus. Mary is told that the name of the child she bears shall be named Jesus, *because he will save his people from their sins* (Matthew 1:21). The one who saves others from sin must be without sin himself.

In a few instances (e.g. Galatians 2:16; Romans 3:22 KJV) the phrase the *faith of Jesus* occurs, which could be rendered the faithfulness of Jesus – his going to the cross as an act of obedience to the Father. Yet even this translation contradicts UR, and it probably should be translated *faith in Jesus* (NIV, NLT, ESV, NASB).

So all the foregoing refutes the claim of universal reconciliation in point 6 above. There is not reconciliation for all humanity, but only personal, individual reconciliation for those who believe the gospel. Young's appeal to church history in point 7 is also a false claim. I demonstrate this in three chapters in my book refuting UR. Those who embrace UR arrogantly assume that they are going to correct the doctrines of the church that it has believed for almost 2,000 years! In appendix 2, I show how one church father, Athanasius, whom Young and Kruger approve, actually writes material that is entirely opposed to UR.

All the foregoing also refutes Young's claims in points 8 through 10. The texts he cites do not support universal salvation, as the contexts make clear. They also run counter to the texts I have just cited here and elsewhere (especially *Lies*, chapter 24). Young's attempt to redefine the "good news" in point 10 is heresy. If people believe UR, they are deceived; they will be lost forever and separated from God. We should define the "good news" as Jesus and the apostles taught it:

> *I want to remind you of the gospel. . . . By this gospel you are saved . . . that Christ died for our sins according to the Scriptures, that he was buried, that he was raised on the third day according to the Scriptures.* (1 Corinthians 15:1-4)

Paul the Apostle explicitly says that it is this gospel which the readers believed and by which they were saved. Note the words *believed* and *were saved*. The Corinthians came out of unbelief by believing in Christ, and this saved them. This text and many others demonstrate that UR is false in its claim that all people are already saved from conception in the womb onward!

Finally, Young should apply his concern for truth in the eleventh point to himself. How can he depart from the faith *once for all delivered to the saints* and expect to escape the judgment of the very hell he denies (Jude 3)? The "lie" of this chapter ("You need to get saved") is not a lie; it is the absolute truth.

If it were a lie, the implications would be staggering. There would never be the need to proclaim the gospel, to do missions work, or to witness to others. The work of Young's own parents was unnecessary; they would have wasted their lives as missionaries. The deaths of all the martyrs for the faith would have been in vain and unnecessary. Yet Paul the Apostle says that the gospel must be preached in order for people to be saved (Romans 10:14-21). He believed that he was obligated to preach the gospel to the whole world (Romans 1:14-17).

Thus, the heart of UR is exposed as an edifice, like "the shack," built on the shifting sands of human opinion without any foundation on the Bible, the Word of God.

CHAPTER 26

"HELL IS SEPARATION FROM GOD"

(*Lies*, chapter 15)

Summary

In this chapter, Young challenges the idea that those in hell are separated from God. He denies that this is the case. But even worse is his slander of God's nature, referring to God as a "torture-devising God," writing that God is unjust for allowing human beings to be in conscious torment for "infinite time" (132). Young devoted several pages to this issue with even more inflammatory language in his paper of 2004. Much of this language is reproduced in the introduction to my book, *Burning Down the Shack*.

Young begins this chapter by telling about growing up in a "religious environment" that spoke of eternal conscious torment and of fear of "hellfire and damnation" (131). He proceeds to give three views of hell: eternal damnation, annihilation, and an age of redemptive purification. Universal reconciliation (UR) and Paul Young propagate the last view. In the rest of the chapter, Young cites the reasons why he believes that this view is best of the three. In the way that he presented the second and third views, he fails to tell us that these views are minor views.

1. Young uses language of emotion and reason to assert that the idea of eternal damnation is unacceptable. He disputes the idea that an "eternally Good God, whose very nature is Love" could allow human beings to be in infinite "conscious torment and pain" (132). Young says it is "intuitively wrong" to be afraid of

a "torture-devising God and yet hope to spend eternity with this God" (132). In Appendix 1, I show how Young expands on this argument.

2. Young seeks to contradict and supplant this view of hell by moving the discussion of hell from the head to the heart.

3. He makes the comparison of a human father with his children, as he did in his novel *The Shack*. He argues that the love people have for their children, such that they could not send any of their children to hell and would choose to go there in place of their children, arises from the love God has for his children.

4. For the rest of the chapter, Young discusses one aspect of hell – separation from God, from Love, Light, and Goodness (134). Young appeals to reason to argue two possibilities to show that hell is not separation from God. One view is that hell is uncreated and thus part of the nature of God; therefore, hell could not be separation from God, but rather in God, who is "Love, Light, Goodness" (134).

The other view is that hell is created. Young then argues that hell cannot be separation from God in light of the promise of Romans 8:38-39, that no "created thing" is able to separate us from the love of God (134). Since people also are created beings, they cannot separate themselves from God. In his novel *Cross Roads*, Young makes a similar claim that hell is not separation from God.[36]

5. Young acknowledges that people may reject or ignore the love of God, and this may become part of their experience and their sense or feelings of separation (Young makes much of this line of reasoning in his novel *Cross Roads*). Yet this experience does not agree with the truth that Young is claiming.

6. If separation from God were true, it means that someone may exist eternally apart from God, who is Life, and apart from

---

36   Wm. Paul Young, *Cross Roads*, 47-48.

the "sustaining life of Jesus" and the Holy Spirit. Yet Scripture (Romans 8), Young claims, prohibits this (136).

7. On the same trajectory of thought, Young suggests that hell is hell not because of the absence of God, but because of the presence of God – the presence "of fiery Love and Goodness and Freedom that intends to destroy every vestige of evil and darkness" that prevents people from being fully alive and free. This fire is forever "for us, not against us," Young argues.

8. Young asserts that hell is "a form of punishment" only if one supposes that it is possible to have existence apart from Jesus (137).

9. Finally, Young proposes that hell is not separation from Jesus, but it is "the pain of resisting our salvation in Jesus while not being able to escape Him who is True Love" (137).

The Biblical Response

The preceding attempt by Young to assert that hell is not separation from God almost takes one's breath away! Note that Young devotes most of this chapter to arguments from reason, with only one biblical text cited (134). The problem with citing the Romans 8 text is that it is not dealing with all humanity, but only with those who are in Christ, who are saved by faith in him (I expand this idea in point 4 below).

Note that in points 1 through 3 Young reverts to what he and other propagators of UR constantly do – appeal to emotional language rather than Scripture. Young excels in this language, as evidenced in his 2004 paper, part of which is cited in the introduction to my *Burning Down the Shack*. He attacks Jesus, as believed in evangelical theology about judgment, as "a million times more vicious and vindictive" than Pharaoh, Nero, and Hitler combined. And here he continues his slander of God by saying that the Christian teaching about torture and pain in hell makes God a "torture-devising God." He describes God and Jesus throughout this chapter as Love, Life, and Good.

But he doesn't reveal two things. First, God also has many other attributes. Second, the Bible associates judgment with both God the Father and with Jesus Christ.

Taking up the first point, I note that from just one text among many we learn of many attributes. Psalm 145 relates that God is good, righteous, slow to anger, loving, compassionate, and faithful, who will care for those who love him but will destroy the wicked (Psalm 145:7-9, 17, 20). David the Psalmist presents a far more balanced understanding of God than Paul Young does.

In the New Testament, God our Father and Jesus Christ are described similarly. Let's consider just two epistles. The Apostle Paul writes to the Thessalonians that God loves believers, who are saved by placing their faith in Christ. *For we know, brothers loved by God . . . your faith in God has become known everywhere* (1 Thessalonians 1:4, 8). Note also 2:14, 16; 3:5-10.

He is the living and true God who rescues believers from "the coming wrath." *They tell how you turned to God from idols to serve the living and true God, and to wait for his Son from heaven, whom he raised from the dead – Jesus, who rescues us from the coming wrath* (1 Thessalonians 1:9-10). God is faithful: *The one who calls you is faithful and he will do it* (1 Thessalonians 5:24). The Apostle reveals both God and Jesus as those who will punish people for sins. *The Lord will punish men for all such sins. . . . Destruction will come on them suddenly, as labor pains on a pregnant woman, and they will not escape* (1 Thessalonians 4:6; 5:3).

Second, the fact that judgment is linked to both God the Father and to Jesus Christ is clearer yet in the next epistle. In 2 Thessalonians, the Apostle writes in his encouraging letter that God is right and just and will bring retribution upon those who are troubling the readers who are believers. The *Lord Jesus* will come from heaven in blazing fire to "punish" those who don't know God and don't obey the gospel. Paul writes powerfully:

> *All this is evidence that God's judgment is right, and as a result you will be counted worthy of the kingdom of God, for which you are suffering. God is just: He will pay back trouble to those who trouble you and give relief to you who are troubled, and to us as well. This will happen when the Lord Jesus is*

revealed from heaven in blazing fire with his powerful angels.
He will punish those who do not know God and do not obey
the gospel of our Lord Jesus. They will be punished with ever-
lasting destruction and shut out from the presence of the Lord
and from the majesty of his power. (2 Thessalonians 1:5-9)

In chapter 2 the Apostle Paul speaks of something that is parallel to what Young is doing in this chapter – seeking to deceive people. Paul warns of people who will try to deceive the Thessalonians about the truth according to the work of Satan. He writes that Satan deceives *in every sort of evil that deceives those who are perishing. They perish because they refused to love the truth and so be saved. For this reason God sends them a powerful delusion so that they will believe the lie and so that all will be condemned who have not believed the truth but have delighted in wickedness* (2 Thessalonians 2:10-12).

The Apostle Paul goes on to commend the readers. *From the begin-ning God chose you to be saved through the sanctifying work of the Spirit and through belief in the truth. He called you to this through our gospel* (2 Thessalonians 2:13-14). Paul then says: *Not everyone has faith. But the Lord is faithful, and he will strengthen and protect you from the evil one* (2 Thessalonians 3:2-3). He commends the readers for their growing faith and love and perseverance and prays that the Lord would direct their hearts *into God's love and Christ's perseverance* (2 Thessalonians 3:5).

How Young Deceives

I have given extra space to cite these texts for several reasons. First, as one reflects on the biblical texts above, it is easy to discover that what Young writes in this chapter is false. The truth is:

1. God is not only love and life but also holy, righteous, and just; and he has other attributes.

2. Both God and Jesus will bring judgment on unbelievers.

3. There are at least two categories of people – those who believe the gospel and those who don't. This statement also contradicts what Young writes about categories in his chapter 5, entitled "God is a Christian."

4. All people are not the objects of God's love and life, but only those who believe the gospel.

5. Faith is absolutely essential for being a child of God.

6. The gospel is clearly defined here as being the truth about Jesus.

7. Christians were chosen from the very beginning, but they had to believe. This represents both the divine side and the human side involved in becoming a Christian.

8. God is not in the presence of the wicked in hell (2 Thessalonians 1:9). Even if God were in hell in some sense, he is not there as love and life, but as holy and just and the Judge who decided their destiny, because they did not choose to believe. It is totally inappropriate for Young in *The Shack* to compare an earthly father's love for his children with God's love for all people. In so doing, Young is placing on Mack, his character, a role that the Bible never places on a human being – to act like God the Judge. No one can ever fulfill God's role in anything. In a sense, this idea is not surprising for one who has constructed God in his own image.

Note how the Bible describes the character of Jesus in similar ways that God the Father is described. We should expect this, for he is the *Son* of God. Indeed, a more complete study of the New Testament reveals that Jesus speaks of hell and judgment four times more frequently than he does of heaven. It is Jesus Christ – not the Apostles Paul, Peter, or John – who uses the strongest terms for the destiny of the lost. For the wicked in hell there is *torment, everlasting fire*, and *everlasting punishment*. He uses other strong language elsewhere, and the Apostle Paul gets his strong language from Jesus Christ!

> *In hell, where he was in torment. . . . Let him warn them,*
> *so that they will not also come to this place of torment.*
> (Luke 16:23, 28)

> *Depart from me, you who are cursed, into the eternal fire*
> *prepared for the devil and his angels. . . . Then they will go*

away to eternal punishment, but the righteous to eternal life.
(Matthew 25:41, 46)

Second, it is without a shadow of doubt that Young and other followers of UR avoid great swaths of the Bible for finding their doctrine about God and how people are saved. Young picks and chooses the texts that seem to support his views. *This is characteristic of all heretics and cults.*

Third, deception from the devil abounds. Shortly after the conversion of the Thessalonians, deception arose. In light of the Bible's complete teaching, it is clear that in his novels and in the movie, Young is a deceiver.

Fourth, consider this. The options are clear. Are we to believe Paul Young and other heretics, or are we to believe Jesus Christ, who experienced death and conquered it, as his apostles reported it?

All the preceding deals with points 1 through 3 above. It also reveals that what Young writes in points 5 through 9 in this chapter is contrary to the Bible. It arises from a depraved mind that puts human reason above the Bible. Note how the Apostle Paul writes about depraved thinking in Romans 1:18-23, 28.

Young's description of hell (point 7) as "fiery love" is similar to his description of hell in his novel *Eve*.[37] There, hell is "purifying fire." Universal reconciliation propagates hell as a temporary place of correction, purification, and cleansing – not an everlasting place of judgment.

It remains for me to deal with point 4 above – the only use that Young makes of Scripture. His appeal to Romans 8 to find justification for his view of hell – that nothing can separate anyone from the love of God – is a false appeal. Several points make this clear. First, the text of Romans 8:28-39 is addressed to believers, as the context of chapter 8 makes clear. Paul the Apostle begins and ends with the assertion that only those in Christ are free from condemnation.

Therefore, there is now no condemnation for those who are in Christ Jesus. (Romans 8:1)

---

37   Wm. Paul Young, *Eve,* 259.

He is addressing believers, who live according to the Spirit, as opposed to those who live according to the flesh and who cannot please God:

> And so he condemned sin in sinful man, in order that the
> righteous requirements of the law might be fully met in us,
> who do not live according to the sinful nature but according to
> the Spirit. Those who live according to the sinful nature have
> their minds set on what that nature desires; but those who live
> in accordance with the Spirit have their minds set on what the
> Spirit desires. The mind of sinful man is death, but the mind
> controlled by the Spirit is life and peace; the sinful mind is
> hostile to God. It does not submit to God's law, nor can it do
> so. Those controlled by the sinful nature cannot please God.
> (Romans 8:3-8)

Believers are those in whom the Spirit dwells and who belong to Christ. *You, however, are controlled not by the sinful nature but by the Spirit, if the Spirit of God lives in you. And if anyone does not have the Spirit of Christ, he does not belong to Christ* (Romans 8:9). They are the true children of God because they are led by the Spirit and have been adopted to sonship, *because those who are led by the Spirit of God are sons of God. . . . And by him we cry, "Abba, Father." The Spirit himself testifies with our spirit that we are God's children. Now if we are children, then we are heirs – heirs of God and co-heirs with Christ* (Romans 8:14-17).

These believers are the children of God who will be key to the liberation of all creation's bondage as they await the redemption of their bodies. *The creation waits in eager expectation for the sons of God to be revealed. For the creation was subjected . . . in hope that the creation itself will be liberated from its bondage to decay and brought into the glorious freedom of the children of God . . . as we wait eagerly for our adoption as sons, the redemption of our bodies* (Romans 8:19-21, 23). In hope, they were saved and have the Spirit to intercede for them. They are God's people who love him and have been called according to his purpose. God foreknew, predestined, called, justified, and will glorify them (Romans 8:24-30).

Do you get the point? The preceding descriptions define a select group who are saved and much more. They are distinguished from the rest of humanity. These same ones are those whom the Apostle Paul says that God is for them and no one can be against them. God gave them Christ as their sacrifice in their stead; they have been given all things. They are chosen, justified, and beyond condemnation. These are the ones who cannot be separated from the love of Christ or *from the love of God in Christ Jesus our Lord* (Romans 8:39).

By applying this text to all people, universally, whether saved or not, Young totally desecrates this powerful encouragement that Christians alone have. Such is the distorted interpretation of UR, which is neither universal nor reconciliation.

Once again, the hermeneutics (interpretation) of UR is uncovered for what it is – distortion.

When Young says at the end of this chapter (point 9) that hell is "the pain of resisting our salvation in Jesus while not being able to escape Him who is True Love," he is speaking universal gibberish (137; see also 187). Hell is far more. It is torment for rejecting the message of the gospel about Jesus Christ, who is with the saints – not with the lost. Jesus promised this torment in Matthew 25:46.

The "lie" of this chapter, "hell is separation from God," is absolutely true. Young is the one who lies when he says that hell does not separate anyone from God.

*CHAPTER 27

"DEATH IS MORE POWERFUL THAN GOD"

(*Lies*, chapter 21)

Summary

This chapter is very important. Young asserts that death does not end the opportunity to change one's destiny. God is more powerful than death and can bring all those in hell to choose love and relationship with him.

With this chapter, we come to one of the chief pillars of universal reconciliation (UR). From a dialogue with friends in a restaurant, Young sets the occasion for addressing whether death is a barrier to any further opportunity for people to change their minds to choose God. He raises the issue by suggesting something that God would never say – namely, "I'm sorry you died. There is nothing I can do for you now. Death wins." Young makes several points in this chapter.

1. Young expands on this idea by saying that God would never say, "Once you die, your fate is sealed, and there is nothing that God can do for you. . . . Your eternal destiny [is] locked" (182).

2. Young suggests that people assume certain ideas are true "because they haven't yet been challenged by life" or by things such as tragedy (183).

3. Young suggests that people have a choice and can change their minds after death.

4. He suggests that the very "intent of judgment is to help us clear away the *lies* [emphasis mine] that are keeping us from making a clear choice" (184).

5. To require people to choose love and relationship prior to death means that "death defines everything" (184). But Young asks, What about people who never knew they had a choice or didn't live long enough to make a choice or were mentally ill or died in the womb?

6. Young goes on to assert that he personally believes that "the idea that we lose our ability to choose at the event of physical death is a significant *lie* [emphasis mine] and needs to be exposed" (185-186). The basis of this, he affirms, is that "love and relationship are possible only when we have the ability to choose" (186).

7. Young argues that evil exists because people turn from "face-to-face relationship with God, and because we chose to say no to God." God submits to the choice of people and goes to incredible lengths to protect people's ability to say no. He then asks, "Why would we think that the event of death would have the power to take away our ability to say yes?" (186).

8. Young asks that if the ability to choose is taken away postmortem (after death), why didn't God "simply take it away to begin with? God could have prevented all this terrible tragedy" (187).

9. Young proposes that "the event of death introduces a crisis (*krisis* – the Greek word, as in the Day of . . . *judgment*), a restorative process intended to free us to run into the arms of Love" (187).

10. Finally, Young believes that children, the mentally ill, the devastated, and the abused will recognize "Love as who God is" and will more readily choose the God of Love than religious people will. Yet, "even for us, Life is bigger than death" (187).

The Biblical Response

This chapter is one of the most critical to UR. At the beginning, Young states that he has thought about the topic in this chapter a long time. Indeed, I note for the reader that Young has been writing about this topic since his 2004 paper, when he strongly asserted that death does not end the opportunity to repent and to be saved from judgment. Young's assertion here that this idea is only a proposal that arose in a recent restaurant dialogue seems quite insincere. I wonder if the whole restaurant dialogue is fictional to gain support for a sympathetic hearing from the unsuspecting and uninformed.

We are dealing here with one of the most essential tenets of UR. Young must affirm what he does about being able "to choose relationship with God" after death if he is going to be true to UR. Universal reconciliation asserts that God's love for all humanity reaches beyond the grave to bring to repentance all who are there and that the fires of hell are purifying and corrective to convince all to choose God. Eventually all go to heaven, and hell ceases to exist. Note in the points below how Young, via his special terminology, comes to this same tenet of UR.

This chapter demonstrates Young's clever attempt to lead the reader step-by-step to doubt the clear teaching of the Bible that there is no longer opportunity to change one's destiny after he/she dies. *And just as man is destined to die once, and after that to face judgment* (Hebrews 9:27). The Bible is totally silent on an opportunity for people to repent after dying and to change their destiny. Indeed, the Bible is not just silent. It teaches the opposite. The parable of the rich man and Lazarus, taught by our Lord Jesus, deliberately says that no one can pass from paradise to hell or from hell to paradise (Luke 16).

Here are the fallacies of Young's case for giving people an opportunity to change their destiny after dying:

(1) He falsely states the issue by saying that "death wins" over God's power. This is a red herring (or even a lie), meant to divert our attention from the real problem. Clearly, the Bible says that Christ's power is greater than death's. Christ's victory over death by his resurrection defeats the power of death. *When the perishable has been clothed with* the imperishable, and the mortal with immortality, then the saying that is written will come true: "Death has been swallowed up in victory." "Where, O death, is your victory? Where, O death, is your sting?" The sting of death is sin, and the power of sin is the law. But thanks be to God! He gives us the victory through our Lord Jesus Christ (1 Corinthians 15:54-57).

Christ freed all believers from the bondage of the fear of death. Since the children have flesh and blood, he too shared in their humanity so that by his death he might destroy him who holds the power of death – that is, the devil – and free those who all their lives were held in slavery by their fear of death (Hebrews 2:14-15). The issue is not about choice, but about the time of choosing, and Scripture limits all choosing to the time prior to death. What if we take Young's view of having a chance to choose after death and a person continues not to choose God after death?

Thus, the real issue is not choice, but making the proper choice at the proper time, as Young well knows. Universal reconciliation allows choice only in one direction – from a place outside of God's favor into it, which is where Young's words are meant to gain a sympathetic hearing.

His words, as cited in summary point 1, are clearly as opposite to what the Bible says as any words could be. God has said just the opposite regarding the meaning and the finality of physical death, as in Hebrews 9:27.

(2) By saying what he does in the second point, Young is basically asserting that experience should determine our theology or doctrine. This is a truly disturbing hermeneutic or basis for interpretation. This approach means that anyone, based on his/her experience, can make the Bible say whatever one wants it to say, and the next person can do the same to a different end. Experience is not our authority for the great issues of life and death, but the Bible is. Note that the basis of all that Young writes in Lies is primarily based on reason and experience; he virtually ignores the Bible. In his novel Cross Roads, Young makes a similar claim that experience is the teacher of truth (Cross Roads, 113). If this is true, then in the end there is no truth, no way, and no life, as found in Jesus Christ, who said, I am the way and the truth and the life. No one comes to the Father except through me (John 14:6).

This exaltation of experience over truth is the great curse of our age and is leading America and Western civilization into the abyss of destruction.

On the other hand, the experience of a certain One should count much. The only One who has gone through death and returned to life evermore is Jesus Christ. His resurrection validates his teaching. Paul Young has no such validation or authority.

(3) The third point rests on no scriptural support. I could assume that giraffes and my dog will go to heaven, and I would have as much biblical support as does Young – which is none. Indeed, even though the Bible is silent on my suggestion, it is not silent regarding Young's view derived from UR. The Bible says there is no chance of changing one's judgment after dying.

> ANIMALS HAVE A GREATER CHANCE OF GOING TO HEAVEN THAN PEOPLE HAVE OF REPENTING AFTER DYING!

(4) This point is Young's way of describing what UR says in other terms. It asserts that the fires of hell are purgatorial and corrective to clear away the resistance to God's love, so that people choose to repent; then they exit hell for heaven. This purpose for suffering is at odds with the expressed purpose for suffering given in Hebrews 12 and Romans 8. Isn't it coercion for God to use the fires of hell to "convince" people to repent? Yet Young denies this. He has a similar discussion in his novel *Cross Roads*.

In my book *Burning Down the Shack*, appendix 4, "The Necessity of the Belief in Hell," I show that from the standpoints of both reason and Scripture, hell and heaven are absolutely necessary.

It is interesting that Young uses "lies" twice in this chapter. This word hardly suggests that Young is making only a proposal. Indeed, using the word "lies" in the title of his book suggests the same strong conviction.

(5) Concerning those who never have a chance to choose is like point

1, and my response is like that in number 1 above. More about these various groups is under number 10 below.

(6) The logic expressed in the second sentence under point 6 seems distorted. The ability to choose love and relationship precedes death for all. All are accountable before they die for their response and for their choice to believe the revelation that God has made in the Bible or in the creation, which is what Paul's letter to the Romans asserts:

> *The wrath of God is being revealed from heaven against all the godlessness and wickedness of men, who suppress the truth by their wickedness, since what may be known about God is plain to them, because God has made it plain to them. For since the creation of the world God's invisible qualities – his eternal power and divine nature – have been clearly seen, being understood from what has been made, so that men are without excuse.* (Romans 1:18-20)

(7) Young defines *evil* as turning from a face-to-face relationship with God and choosing to say no to God as Life, Light, Truth, and Good. Yet the Bible defines evil much more strongly – as sin, coming short of the mark of God's standard of perfect righteousness, and as open hostility toward God, as described in Colossians: *Once you were alienated from God and were enemies in your minds because of your evil behavior* (Colossians 1:21).

Further, "turning away from relationship" is Young's characteristic way of describing the fall of Adam in his novel *Eve.* Yet "turning away" is quite muted next to the Bible's terms of transgression and trespass (which assume violation of a boundary), rebellion, evil, iniquity, guilt, perversity, disobedience, and sin. In actual usage, the Bible rarely uses the idea of turning away.

The Apostle Paul also wrote to the Ephesians about their past hostility: *As for you, you were dead in your transgressions and sins, in which you used to live when you followed the ways of this world and of the ruler of the kingdom of the air, the spirit who is now at work in those who are disobedient. All of us also lived among them at one time, gratifying the cravings of our sinful nature and following its desires and thoughts. Like the rest, we were by nature objects of wrath* (Ephesians 2:1-3).

Romans 5:12 also speaks of death coming to all men because of Adam's sin: *Therefore, just as sin entered the world through one man, and death through sin, and in this way death came to all men, because all sinned.*

I also note that Young's use of capitals in his definition of God is questionable, and he fails to note that God is also holy, just, righteous, and salvation (Psalm 27:1). Without acknowledging these attributes, Young has created a truncated deity who is not the God of the Bible.

Where do we discover the attributes of God? Young finds them in human beings and in experience, which seems to be making gods out of human beings. But our primary source and the only truly authoritative source is the Bible. Note that in an earlier chapter I emphasized Psalm 145 and the Thessalonian epistles.

Also, in point 7 Young is again asserting that people's ability to choose love and relationship should continue after death; death should not be an obstacle to this choice. Yet there is no biblical support for this. Young appeals to reason and emotion without the necessary biblical support.

Following Young's logic, why shouldn't God continue to protect people's ability to say no to God's love and relationship (Young's terms) throughout eternity? But this runs counter to the tenet of UR that none must be left in the universe who are outside of God's love as expressed in heaven. Thus, UR is very deterministic; in the end it does not respect the free choice of people to *dis*believe.

(8) The Bible's teaching is what is at stake here. In Genesis 3, the Bible teaches that God gave people the ability to choose to obey or not to obey, and he continues to offer people this opportunity now to believe in Christ. The Bible denies this opportunity after death (as noted above). People can speculate all they want, but when such speculation violates the revelation of the Bible, then speculations are in error. Of course, Young seems unconstrained by the Bible.

People can speculate all they want about the future, but whose speculation is correct and should really count? Only Jesus Christ has the credentials, by his resurrection, to support his claim to know what lies beyond the grave.

(9) Young's citation of the Greek *krisis* adds nothing to the discussion. There is no basis for connecting the word with a restorative process through our English "crisis." Young comes closest here to talking about judgment, a word that proponents of UR are loath to use, since God is love. Notice that he refers to the "purgatorial fires" of UR by much milder words: "a restorative process intended to free us to run."

(10) This point is a very important matter. Young and other proponents of UR fault Christians for allowing the various categories of people to get to heaven without being saved by placing faith in Jesus Christ. They accuse Christians of being inconsistent. In his paper of 2004, Young was particularly abrasive about this matter. He asserted that the view of Christians is that there will be many more billions in hell than will be in heaven.

But this view is in error. Generally, Christians have always taken the position that the groups that Young names have heaven as their destiny. With the support of Scripture, they appeal to the nature of God as both loving and just. And amazingly, the numbers who will be in heaven will far, far exceed those in hell. I've recently written on this matter.[38]

Before I bring this chapter to a close, it is important to recognize what Young has done here. He has embraced the basic tenet of UR, that death does not end the opportunity to find a relationship with God.

But note also that what Young says here is in contradiction to what he has said elsewhere. He has claimed that all are already saved (chapter 13); all are God's children (chapter 24); hell and sin do not separate from God (chapters 15 and 27); and God is good (chapters 2 and 16). Why should people experience hell, even for a little while, if they already are what is described in the other chapters – that they are already God's children?

Note that Young never uses the word *hell* in this chapter. He simply says that after death, people should have the opportunity to choose love

---

38   See my paper, "The Sledgehammer of Universalism: Few Will Be in Heaven but Billions Will Be in Hell" (March 2017), available on my website, burningdowntheshackbook.com.

and relationship with God. Apparently, it is only an assumption on our part that this means that people are in hell and not in the presence of God after death (or perhaps they are in heaven! But then it would be unnecessary to pen this chapter). So, where are people, when considering all the "lies" that Young states in all his chapters? Perhaps the best answer is that they are in purgatory. But Young would probably not embrace Roman Catholic doctrine. Roman Catholic doctrine states that purgatory is only for correcting or purging Christians; it is not a place to give a second chance to unbelievers to repent and change their destiny.

What a theological quagmire! The "lie" of this chapter is a straw man. No Christian believes that death is more powerful than God. By his resurrection, Jesus has conquered death and proves that death is no longer a terror to Christians, as explicitly affirmed in Romans 8:38-39 and in 1 Corinthians 15:54-56: *Death has been swallowed up in victory.*

CHAPTER 28

"SIN SEPARATES US FROM GOD"

(*Lies*, chapter 27)

Summary

In chapter 27 of his book, Young addresses one of the most important topics of Christian doctrine. He defines *sin* in his unique way and denies that it means separation from God. Young's universal reconciliation (UR) is strongly in place here.

Young boldly takes on one of the central teachings of Christian faith as he seeks to define sin as something other than what Christians have always believed. He claims that sin's effect is not to separate anyone from God.

Young first deals with what sin is. He talks about how his novel *The Shack* has helped people seek healing for their broken hearts, yet they think that they can't be in relationship with God because of some behavior or shame in their past.

1. Young remarks that their "actions never had the power to separate them from God in the first place" (225).

2. Young says that people make "mistakes" as an "essential part of being human," but these are not the "same as sinning" (226).

3. He identifies pride as a sin because it is a "denial of being human" (227).

4. Young then considers whether "active rebellion, betrayal, and hurting others and ourselves" is sin. He suggests that sin is not

"fundamentally about behavior, but something deeper" (227). He reveals that the "actual disease" is discovered by noting that the Greek word *hamartia* does not mean "missing the mark," as though the mark is "moral perfection or moral behavior," because this idea of performance is wrong. Since the essence of "God's nature is relationship," then sin must be understood as "missing a relational reality" (228).

5. To understand what this idea means, Young appeals to the Greek word as made up of two parts: *ha-* meaning "no" or a negation, and *-martia*, from the Greek root *meros*, meaning "form, origin, or being" (228). So the meaning of the Greek word is "negation of origin or being" or "formlessness." Thus, sin means that one is "missing the mark" of the "Truth of your being" (229).

6. Young defines the truth of the being of people, who they are, as their being "very good" as God proclaimed at the end of the sixth day of creation in Genesis 1 (229). Sin, then, is anything that diminishes the truth of who people are. Behavior then becomes either an authentic way of expressing the truth of people's good creation, or a behavior to cover up the shame of what people think about themselves, i.e., worthless. Apparently, Young suggests here that people can look either to the record of creation or to themselves.

7. What does the truth of the being of people look like? Young answers: "God." People are made in the image of God, and the truth of "being looks like God" (229). He then cites a list of good qualities that reflect primarily the fruit of the Spirit and the description of love (Galatians 5:22-23; 1 Corinthians 13).

8. Young devotes the second part of the chapter to a discussion of whether sin separates from God. He faults Christians for espousing "a theology of separation," so that, as with other religions, an entire system and institution "can be built as the path to salvation" (231). He says that it is a "lie" to affirm that

the following statement is in the Bible when it isn't: "You have sinned, and you are separated from God" (231).

9. With this theology of separation comes "devastating implications" and "unanswerable questions" (231). How does one get unseparated? What do I have to do or say to get across the great divide and "be made part of the 'special people'"? How does one know when one is "in" or "across"? Is it temporary? What if people don't know how to get across? Christians can't agree on what it means for Jesus to get people across or how he did it or for whom (231).

10. Separation "is a lie"; "no one has ever been separated from God. That is exactly what it means" (232). Young cites Romans 8:38-39 here (as he did to refute the "lie" of his chapter 15). So Jesus did not come to "build a bridge back to God," but to show people who "are lost in the delusion of separation" the example of a life who "knows He is not" (232).

11. As support for the preceding, Young remarks that there is nothing "outside God. There is only God, and Creation is created 'in God' . . . specifically 'inside Jesus,' the Word who is God" (232). Young appeals to John 1:3-4 here.

12. Jesus is "actually and historically God fully joining us in our humanity. . . . Then Jesus is God comfortable in His own skin. . . . He is God in the midst of . . . our brokenness and blindness" (232).

13. Young concludes by asking whether we people, who may be "horrific" in how we behave, or are so "wretched," "sinful," and "abhorrent," are "powerful enough . . . to push God away" (232). Young observes that God is not ever distant. "There is no separation" (233).

The Biblical Response

Wow! The brazenness that Young expresses in point 10 reminds me of the same way he expressed his confession of being a universalist (118).

Here again there is absolutely no doubt that Young imbibes universal reconciliation (UR). There is much to respond to here – first regarding what sin is, and then whether sin separates one from God. Young is deeply in error on both issues.

(1) Young will later try to prove the first point, even by citing Scripture – though wrongly, I might add. Adam and Eve's actions did separate them from God, as Genesis 3 clearly shows. The two hid themselves from God, and thereby symbolized their spiritual distance because of disobedience. Then God cast them out of the Garden of Eden.

(2) This point is correct; there is a difference between mistakes and sins. Yet Young never discusses the real difference as Christians have viewed it. Many mistakes carry no moral culpability and guilt as violations of God's Word, his law, and his nature, while some mistakes may carry some of each. Indeed, there are often consequences for mistakes. Yet all sins always carry moral culpability and guilt, and do come with serious repercussions, both here on earth, and later when we meet God. When Young comes to defining sin, he clearly doesn't like these distinctions.

(3) Young's definition of pride is somewhat erroneous. Although he speaks of pride as a denial of being human, he says nothing of the fact that it is also arrogant redefinition constituting rebellion against God (placing the creature over the Creator). Pride is not just the sin of omission (denying one's humanity), but also of commission (trying to be God). Both Satan and Adam in the garden left their God-given roles and tried to be *as God* (Genesis 3). In like manner, Christ was tempted in the wilderness – tempted to worship Satan instead of God (Matthew 4). Young's trivializing of pride highlights again that the tenets of UR revolve around the creature instead of the Creator.

(4) There are several errors of Young's beliefs recorded under the fourth point. First, Young is wrong in asserting that sin is not "fundamentally about behavior, but something deeper." It is actually both. Christian doctrine professes that humanity has fallen in Adam's sin and thus

partakes of a nature that is depraved or sinful (Romans 5:12). In addition, this fallen nature leads to the commission of individual sins or behavior over the lifetime of an individual. Thus, human beings are guilty of both having a sin nature and committing acts of sin. Both make people guilty before God and cause them to be in need of atonement and forgiveness by the death of Christ. *For all have sinned and fall short of the glory of God, and are justified freely by his grace through the redemption that came by Christ Jesus. God presented him as a sacrifice of atonement, through faith in his blood. He did this to demonstrate his justice, because in his forbearance he had left the sins committed beforehand unpunished* (Romans 3:23-25).

Second, Young is wrong in defining *hamartia* as "missing a relational reality." It is this, but it is much more. He is wrong in making *hamartia* refer to performance – to the doing of "moral perfection or moral behavior" to the exclusion of character or nature. Morality is involved again, not only as a flaw in behavior, but also in human nature. Primarily, the word does mean missing the mark of God's perfection, God's absolute holiness, but sin is also failing to do what God commands – absolute obedience to his law without a single blemish.

(5) Regarding his word study, Young is wrong to appeal to the etymology of a word (*hamartia*) to get its meaning. He claims it is from *ha-*, meaning "no," and from *-martia*, from the root word *meros*, meaning "being." Hence, he defines it as "no being" or "formlessness." This is questionable. First, the etymology of this word is uncertain.[39] Young's idea to define it relative to a person's being is an arbitrary extrapolation. Second, all linguists using the Greek New Testament point to the fallacy of getting final meaning from etymology. Instead, context determines meaning. Young states that the meaning is "missing the mark" of the "truth of one's being." No New Testament context supports Young's idea.

Sin, from *hamartia,* does mean to miss the mark of the moral perfection

---

39   Some suggest it comes from a word (*hamartia*) meaning "failing to grasp" or from a word (*meros*) meaning "having a share of"; hence "not having a share of" or "miss" (see R. C. Trench, *Trench's Synonyms of the New Testament* [Grand Rapids: Eerdmans, rep. 1966], 240). The context must tell what it is that is being "missed." Young arbitrarily links it to what a person misses in his being. In any case, *all* reputable lexicons and dictionaries note that in the NT the term consistently is used theologically and morally of people's falling short of God's standard. Young is totally without support.

of the nature of God and his law – to *come short of the glory of God*. No Greek dictionary gives the definition of *hamartia* that Young asserts!

If Young is correct, what would "sinning against God" mean? Further, how does Young's idea fit the parallel words in Romans 3:23: *and come short of the glory of God*? And how does his meaning fit Romans 6:23: *the wages of sin* [supposedly, missing the mark or truth of one's being] *is death*? Young's redefinition orients the offense toward people rather than toward God. As mentioned before, UR remakes God in the image of human beings. So even the focus of sin is on what it means regarding people, and not on what it means regarding God. Young says people are wrong in their thinking about themselves, not wrong in their thinking about God. No reputable Bible scholar would ever define sin this way.[40] On the contrary, David seemed to understand what sin was when he wrote, *For I know my transgressions, and my sin is always before me. Against you, you only, have I sinned and done what is evil in your sight, so that you are proved right when you speak and justified when you judge* (Psalm 51:4).

Young seems to be revitalizing the older, general concept of sin being a missing of the target or being a defect of character, as found in non-biblical usage. He departs from the stronger, biblical sense where the term always involves an offense against God, whether people are involved or not. Thus, murder not only harms a person, but it also violates God's law.

(6) The previous comments are appropriate for point 6 as well. The so-called "truth of the being" of people as "very good" applies to people only through the record of Genesis 1 and 2. Note that Young said that people are "fundamentally good" (34). In Genesis 3 the whole human race is plunged into sin so much that human beings are "fundamentally bad," and all died in Adam. If the rebellion of Adam and Eve against God was not so bad, why did Adam and Eve die? Why did all humanity die with/in them? And why does the Apostle Paul teach that *there is no*

---

40   Gunther is representative. *Hamartia* is "always used in the NT of man's sin which is ulti-mately directed against God" (W. Gunther, "Sin," *The New International Dictionary of NT Theology* [Grand Rapids: Zondervan, 1978] 3:579).

one righteous, not even one, and that the *whole world is held accountable to God*? (Romans 3:10, 19).

In the Garden of Eden, sin was not "diminishing the truth of who people are" as Young claims, but it was diminishing the truth of who God is! The two believed Satan's lie that attacked the character of God. People come *short of the glory of God,* not short of the truth of being human! The only remedy is the gift of righteousness from an outside source, from God, as the Apostle writes: Righteousness is *given through faith in Jesus Christ to all who believe* (Romans 3:22).

Young carries his unbiblical idea about sin to an interesting application for living. He has said that "wholeness is when the way of our being matches the truth of our being."[41] Yet how can there be a legitimate or helpful application for life when the definition of sin is distorted?

(7) For Young to say that the "truth of being looks like God," since people are made in his image, ignores the fall recorded in Genesis 3 that deeply corrupted the image and the qualities it produces. What Young cites as good qualities come about because of the work of God – the fruit produced by the Spirit in believers (Galatians 5:22-23). Left to themselves, humans cannot do one thing to make themselves spiritually acceptable to God. *All* have sinned and **come short** of the glory of God (Romans 3:23, author's emphasis).

Further, YOUNG'S DEFINITION OF SIN IS PERILOUSLY CLOSE TO THE GREAT LIE OF SATAN IN THE GARDEN OF EDEN (Genesis 3). Satan the serpent deceived Eve and Adam with the lie that they would become as God. Young's allurement is that the truth of people's being would "look like God." He is saying that the nature of people would be like God's nature!

(8) Young slanders Christianity for making it like any other religion and accusing it of teaching a "theology of separation." This is false. Christianity embraces a theology of forgiveness and acceptance of all in the *body of Christ* (1 Corinthians 2:27; note also Colossians 3:11). His anti-institutional bent comes through again (*Lies,* chapters 11-12)

41   This statement was made by Young when he was interviewed by Oprah Winfrey on July 6, 2017 (uploaded on wpy.wmpaulyoung.com, July 13, 2017).

as he condemns Christianity for building a system and institution that defines the "path of salvation." Clearly Young rebels against the exclusive claims of Jesus Christ as the only way to God (John 14:6). The Christian church is only following Jesus in this regard. The church is not an institution created by early Christians. Jesus Christ claimed to be the builder of the church, forming one new group on the foundation of the apostles and prophets. Jesus told Peter regarding his confession, *And I tell you that you are Peter, and on this rock I will build my church* (Matthew 16:18). Paul also told the Ephesians, *For he himself is our peace, who has made the two one and has destroyed the barrier. . . . His purpose was to create in himself one new man out of the two. . . . Consequently, you are no longer foreigners and aliens, but fellow citizens with God's people and members of God's household, built on the foundation of the apostles and prophets, with Christ Jesus himself as the chief cornerstone* (Ephesians 2:14-15, 19-20).

For Young to reject the church, which is both an institution and an organism, he must <u>reject the Lord Jesus as the cornerstone of it</u>!

For Young to assert that the words "You have sinned, and you are separated from God" are not in the Bible is in error. Certainly, to *come short of the glory of God* means to be separated from God. And what would Young do with this verse: *Your iniquities have made a separation between you and your God, and your sins have hidden his face from you so that he does not hear* (Isaiah 59:2 ESV)? And this: the Gentiles walk *in the futility of their minds. They are darkened in their understanding, alienated from the life of God* (Ephesians 4:17-18 ESV). Young is flat-out wrong on this!

(9) All the questions that Young raises in this point go away if evangelical theology, which strives to follow the apostles in understanding the gospel, is embraced. While there is not total agreement in evangelical theology on many minor points (Young says Christians can't agree), there is agreement on all the big issues that Young deals with in his book, *Lies*. On these issues, his attempt to drive a wedge among Christians is futile.

(10) This is Young's bold assertion that it is a lie that anyone has ever been separated from God, and "that is exactly what it means." This is itself a lie. The preceding discussion is the basis for calling his statement a lie. For Young to find support in Romans 8:38-39 is an incorrect use of Scripture, for the text applies only to Christians, as the context shows (as I also wrote when dealing with *Lies*, chapter 15).

For Young to write that Jesus is not a bridge back to God is a slander of the Lord Jesus who said, *I am the way. . . . No one comes to the Father except through me* (John 14:6). Young calls the Christian proclamation of this unique distinctive of Jesus as the way of salvation for the lost "a delusion." But Young is delusional. While Jesus may not have used the figure of a bridge, he did say that he is the bread of life (John 6:35-51), the light of the world (John 8:12; 9:5), the door (John 10:7-9), the good shepherd (John 10:11-14), the resurrection and the life (John 11:25), the only way to God (John 14:6), and the true vine (John 15:1). He insisted on the necessity of believing in him (John 8:24; 9:35-41).

(11) Young finds his support for saying that no one has ever been separated from God by going to the creation account. He maintains that all of creation, including humans, is created "in God." This is heresy. Such a view leads to pantheism (everything is God) and the destruction of God's transcendence (supremacy). God is above and beyond his creation. Only Christians who have accepted Christ are in Christ, by virtue of their believing in Christ. Paul explains this to the Ephesians:

> *Remember that at that time you were separate from Christ,*
> *excluded from citizenship in Israel and foreigners to the*
> *covenants of the promise, without hope and without God in*
> *the world. But now in Christ Jesus you who once were far*
> *away have been brought near through the blood of Christ.*
> (Ephesians 2:12-13)

Young's appeal to John 1:3-4, that in Christ *was life, and that life was the light of men*, is meant to support the idea that all humanity has life. Yet the very next verses limit this life to all who believe:

> *He came as a witness to testify concerning that light, so that*

through him all men might believe. . . . Yet to all who received
him, to those who believed in his name, he gave the right to
become children of God. (John 1:7, 12)

(12) Young affirms that Jesus became fully human and joined the race in its brokenness and blindness. The latter terms come from Young's assessment that human beings are fundamentally good, but are only blind to their being children of God already – from birth. There is no need for anyone to "accept Christ" to be saved, because all are already saved (the substance of *Lies*, chapter 13). With such words, Young denies people the opportunity to be transformed by the new birth, to be redeemed/rescued from the penalty and power of sin, to have sins forgiven and guilt removed, and to find peace with God. Young's theology has no place for transformation.[42]

(13) Young asserts that no one is "powerful enough to push God away," to make God distant, or to be separated from him. His universal reconciliation is in the background here, for according to UR, none will experience separation from God. Under point 8, I presented verses that affirm that sin separates people who are unrepentant from God. People are responsible for their choice of spurning the offer of life and forgiveness in the gospel. In this sense, they "push God away." God does not force on people something contrary to what they choose. God abides by the choice of will that he gave to people.

The "lie" that Young affirms in this chapter, "sin separates us from God," is not a lie. It is the absolute truth.

It is fitting that Young's chapter 27 should be the last chapter in my arrangement of his "lies." The "lie" of this chapter is one of the core doctrines of Christian theology. If sin and separation are redefined as Young asserts here, there is no need for the death and resurrection of Christ.

This is not just my conclusion. Others who have written to expose universal reconciliation have noted that this heresy goes to the heart

---

42   Indeed, as late as July of 2017 in his interview with Oprah Winfrey, Young said that one
      does not need to experience a "transformation but an uncovering of who I already am"
      (see www.wmpaulyoung.com).

of the gospel.[43] If people can be saved without believing the gospel, then Jesus Christ did not have to give his life on the cross. He died in vain. And note that this is what Young asserts as a "lie" in his chapter 17: "The cross was God's idea." It was, he says, man's idea – not God's.

---

43 Note as one among many, William G. T. Shedd, *The Doctrine of Endless Punishment* (New York: Scribner's Sons, 1886; rep. 1980), p. vi: "The rejection of the doctrine of Endless Punishment cuts the ground from under the gospel. . . . No error, consequently, is more fatal than that of Universalism."

CONCLUSION

ADDITIONAL MATTERS, OBSERVATIONS, AND QUESTIONS

SOME ADDITIONAL MATTERS

Paul Young concludes his book, *Lies We Believe about God*, by making two more attempts to convert the reader to universal reconciliation (UR). First, he provides a list, a catena, of about thirty-four biblical texts that he thinks support UR. This is not the first time Young has provided such a list. In his paper of 2004, he listed a multitude of such texts. How does one respond to such a list? Here are some observations.

Virtually all the texts involve the words *all*, *whole*, *every*, or their equivalents. The point is that Young wants to take such texts universally. The replies to this idea are as follows:

1. Some instances of the chosen word are limited in the immediate context to a number less than all.

2. Some instances are limited in a wider context to a lesser number.

3. Some other texts are limited by the entire teaching of the New Testament where there are statements that say just the opposite, or limit or qualify the statements. A writer of the New Testament cannot be in contradiction to himself, such that he means "all" in one point and "not all" in another.

4. At least one text is immediately limited, so that *all* means "those who believe."

Suffice it to say that I have dealt with virtually all of these texts and more, both in my reply to Young's 2004 paper, which is available on my website *burningdowntheshackbook.com*, and in my forthcoming book. No one reading *Lies* should be shaken by Young's list. For every text that Young uses, there is a legitimate response that agrees with evangelical faith. If this were not the case, Christian history would have succumbed to UR long ago. Instead, it has consistently exposed the inadequacies of UR to a watching, Christian world.

The second way by which Young seeks to convert readers at the end of his book is by citing well-known Christians who seemingly think the way he does – as a champion of UR.

He cites "A Final Word from Dietrich Bonhoeffer." Bonhoeffer was a German pastor and writer who was put to death by the Nazis on April 9, 1945. Christians have long appreciated Bonhoeffer's desire to know God deeply. Young cites several paragraphs from Bonhoeffer's book, *Ethics*.

In this piece there are statements that hint of UR, but these could be taken as the biblical statements that I dealt with above. My research has concluded that while Bonhoeffer may have had some UR tendencies, no one can conclude that he was a follower of UR. He was certainly not in the camp with Young and all his slander of the Bible. My consultation with a recent biographer, Joel Burnell, who wrote *Poetry, Providence, and Patriotism: Polish Messianism in Dialogue with Dietrich Bonhoeffer*, agrees with this assessment.[44]

Last of all, Young appeals to other names who have helped him in the writing of his ideas and in support of him. He first expresses gratitude for "early church fathers and mothers" who "enlarged and deepened" his "view of Jesus." Apparently, we are to infer that these people support his ideas in *Lies*. Nothing could be further from the truth. On the major issues raised in *Lies*, virtually all church fathers espoused the same beliefs that evangelical Christianity does today. See the appendix on the church father, Athanasius, for a sparkling example.

Young cites other people who agree with him and who have helped with his ideas. At the end, he thanks C. Baxter Kruger and John MacMurray for their help. See the appendix about Kruger's evaluation of Young's orthodoxy.

---

44   Joel Burnell, *Poetry, Providence, and Patriotism: Polish Messianism in Dialogue with Dietrich Bonhoeffer* (Eugene, OR: Pickwick Publications, 2009).

SOME SOBER OBSERVATIONS

Some observations regarding *Lies We Believe about God* and its author, Paul Young:

Despite a few attempts at qualification, Paul Young is not reluctant to write as a true believer in universal reconciliation (UR). Note that he confesses this unequivocally in chapter 13.

The topics of all of these chapters could have given Young the opportunity to help Christians grow. Instead, he subverts the primary beliefs of Christianity. He attacks beliefs that are not merely tangential (secondary) to the Christian faith, but he goes for the jugular in about half of his book (chapters 2, 3, 4, 7, 10, 13, 15, 17, 19, 21, 24, 27, and 28). If people follow Young, evangelical faith will be overthrown. Young seems to encourage this.

Young is out to convince others to follow him. He repeatedly uses "lies" not only in the titles of every chapter and in the title of the book, but many times throughout the text (pages 177, 184, 186, 211, 214, and 215, for example). He continues down the same path of UR that he began in his forum paper of 2004 and continued in *The Shack*, *Cross Roads*, and *Eve*. At the least Young is consistent in his devotion to this heresy.

I believe that he is emboldened by the extraordinary sales of his books and the success of the film. He has influenced millions, and he makes note of this in several chapters (see 18, 20, 22, 23, and others). He lauds the success of his novels and movie and he is unconcerned by the negative response that mainline Christians and evangelicals have to his writing.

I believe that Young is motivated by his belief that the structures of the evangelical church are failing, and he is projecting a new form of Christianity, as he states in the interview from *Religious News Service* (March 3, 2017) and the recent interview with Kruger online at *Perichoresis*. His beliefs are only slightly related to the Bible. See the appendix below.

It seems that Young is formulating a new "scripture," a canon within the Canon, the authoritative books of the Bible. He is deceptive in what he writes and what he says in public meetings:

1. He fails to acknowledge his past cover-ups of what he truly

believes – that he is a committed believer in universal reconciliation (118).

2. He fails to acknowledge that his life was turned around by his
conversion to UR, as he claims in his 2004 paper. For thirteen
years he has not deviated from what he says in this paper, as
slanderous of God and of Christians though it may be.

3. As revealed in his autobiographical notes, he is still in a position of rebellion against God that began in early childhood, and
against his parents and his upbringing. He has not resolved his
discord with his father (210).

Young constantly uses a personal experience in order to validate his
novel claims to truth, when it seems that the Bible might oppose what
he writes (47). There are significant omissions in Young's practice and
writing:

1. He has little place for the devil and his influence in the world,
yet Jesus called him the *prince of this world* (John 16:11) and Paul
the Apostle often warned about the devil (Ephesians 6:11-12).

2. He gives no attention to the ordinances of baptism and the
Lord's Supper (Communion). In so doing, he does not obey
our Lord's command to obey him and remember him.

3. He attends no church (as far as I know) and thus does not come
under any authority of church elders and leaders (Hebrews 13:7,
17). His commitment to UR seems to prevent this.

4. He has said virtually nothing about the return of Christ and
the Second Coming. Does he even believe it? Jesus's return is
the *blessed hope* of Christians (1 Thessalonians 5:23; Titus 2:13).

FIVE HEAVY QUESTIONS

1. Should we pray for Young to repent and come back to God?
I don't know. It is a dilemma. I can't find a text in Scripture that either
exhorts or models this kind of praying. Our Lord does exhort us to love
our enemies, but in this same Sermon on the Mount he warns of *false*

prophets and those who profess that they know him but by their works show that they don't (Matthew 5:44). These are "evil doers" (Matthew 7:15-23). While the apostles often indict or warn about false teachers (Galatians 1; 2 Corinthians 11; Philippians 1:15-17, 3:2, 18-20; Colossians 2:16-19; 1 John 4; Jude), they never exhort prayer for them.

2. Can Young repent and change?

This question is also a dilemma, but I don't think so. I cannot find examples in the Bible of heretics who repented. Instead, the biblical record is quite revealing and negative. Very early on, the Apostle Paul in 1 and 2 Timothy identified Hymenaeus and Alexander who had shipwrecked regarding the faith (1 Timothy 1:19-20); certain widows who had turned away to follow Satan (5:15); money seekers who had wandered from the faith (6:10); seekers of false knowledge who departed from the faith (6:21); Phygelus and Hermogenes who had deserted Paul (2 Timothy 1:15) and departed from the truth (2:17-18); men of depraved minds who were rejected regarding the faith (3:8); Demas who deserted Paul (4:10); and Alexander who opposed Paul and against whom Paul sought retribution from the Lord (4:14-15). In Acts 8, Simon the sorcerer was condemned by Peter; subsequent church history portrayed him as an ongoing opponent of the Apostle Peter. Also, Paul the Apostle warns of eternal perdition to come on those who *preach a gospel other than the one* he preached (Galatians 1:7-9).

This biblical record is not dealing with persecutors or opponents of the gospel (except perhaps for Alexander). Instead, these are people who once knew the truth of the gospel, then rejected it. Young has gone so far in his desertion from evangelical faith, he has been so successful, he is so deeply pursued by millions as their "spiritual guru," he has become so inventive and creative among the advocates of UR, and he has been so consistent in defending UR, that from a human/natural standpoint it seems unlikely that he will ever repent.

The Bible says that for such apostates it is *impossible to renew them again to repentance* (Hebrews 6:6). The writer of Hebrews goes on to say:

> *If we deliberately keep on sinning after we have received the knowledge of the truth, no sacrifice for sins is left, but only a*

*fearful expectation of judgment and of raging fire that will
consume the enemies of God. Anyone who rejected the law of
Moses died without mercy on the testimony of two or three
witnesses. How much more severely do you think a man
deserves to be punished who has trampled the Son of God
under foot, who has treated as an unholy thing the blood of the
covenant that sanctified him, and who has insulted the Spirit
of grace? . . . See to it that you do not refuse him who speaks. If
they did not escape when they refused him who warned them
on earth, how much less will we, if we turn away from him
who warns us from heaven?* (Hebrews 10:26-31; 12:25)

The preceding Scriptures should sober every Christian. I have to wonder about Young's impact on his family and all those who follow him.

It is heart-wrenching to see a former friend who I once thought was
a Christian now become a chief heretic, leading others astray.

3. What should the Christian church do? How should it respond?
There is no dilemma here. The church needs to recognize that there is
a great danger from universal reconciliation. If it were true, the death
of Christ would have been unnecessary. Christians need to grasp the
reality that the evangelical church is on a trajectory of novelty, corruption in doctrine and practice, and indifference toward the history of the
church and doctrine. The church must expose the error of universalism
and its proponents.

4. Is Wm. P. Young forming a new cult?
In light of the preceding comments, Paul Young and his followers fit
the description of a cult.[45] He is a charismatic leader. He puts his story
and the distortion of universal reconciliation over the clear teaching of
the Bible and the Christian Church. He opposes the traditional church.
He views himself as a leader of a new reformation (and others agree).
He has followers numbering in the millions. There is a lot of money

---

45   Among other ideas, the *Webster's New World Dictionary* (3rd College Ed., 1988) defines
      "cult" as a" quasi-religious group with a charismatic leader who indoctrinates members
      with unorthodox or extremist views, practices, or beliefs." It involves "devoted attachment
      to, or extravagant admiration for a person, principle, or lifestyle" (337).

involved. There is an interest in the sexual nature of God. He pursues his own peculiar and extreme form of universal reconciliation.

What else is necessary to be a cult? Only time! Jude writes his brief letter to expose false teachers already appearing within the first century. Part of it seems appropriate for Paul Young and his followers, such as verses 3-4, 17-19.

5. Is Paul Young Leading a "New Reformation"?

Paul Young's admirer, C. Baxter Kruger, suggests that Young may be a new Martin Luther (see the Introduction, p. xvi). Paul Young himself has suggested that he is on the cusp of a "new reformation" (see the Introduction, p. xvii). Is this possible? Is it probable?

No, it is not. I am writing this book during the 500th anniversary of the Protestant Reformation. In light of his multiple departures from biblical teaching Paul Young is not leading what he calls a "new reformation." The battle cry of the Reformation of Martin Luther, Philip Melancthon, Ulrich Zwingli, and John Calvin was "sola scriptura" – the Scriptures alone. On the ultimate authority of the Bible alone they were willing to take their stand, and now 500 years later, their witness has stood the test of time.

It is not a "new reformation" that Young leads or hopes for, but an old revolt against the authority of the Bible and the words of Jesus Christ. Jesus promised: *I will build my church and the gates of hell shall not prevail against it* – and this promise includes the work of Paul Young and all other heretics that rejects the clear teaching from Jesus and the apostles about heaven and hell.

APPENDIX 1

IS PAUL YOUNG'S CLAIM TRUE THAT HIS BELIEFS ARE ORTHODOX BY THE NICENE CREED?

Readers of this exposé of *Lies* will probably be surprised that in spite of all that I've written about Young's aberrant theology, Paul Young himself says that his beliefs are orthodox, or biblical. In an interview recorded on the website of C. Baxter Kruger, Kruger puts several questions to Young which concern Young's orthodoxy.[46]

Young's Answers about His Orthodoxy

Kruger asks Young six questions:

(1) When asked if he is a heretic, Paul Young answers, "Of course not." He says that orthodoxy is defined by "Athanasius and the Nicene Creed. I stand with the Creed."

Earlier in the interview, Kruger had said that *The Shack* reminded him of Athanasius, who said, "The God of all is good, and supremely noble by nature. Therefore, He is the lover of the human race." Kruger expresses his opinion that Paul Young is "a lover of the Nicene Creed"; that "Paul Young is as orthodox as St. Athanasius, whose work in the early church set the definition of orthodoxy and thus of heresy as well." In this appendix and another we'll examine whether or not Kruger's assessment is true. We'll find that it is not.

Young goes on to elaborate on the answer to the first question. He notes that he understands how the Nicene Creed came to be, and he

---

46   "William Paul Young: Orthodox Novelist," *Perichoresis: www.perichoresis.org* (Feb. 28, 2017).

"definitely agrees with its heart." I'm not sure what this statement means; it appears to be a qualification or limitation. He acknowledges that he is not sure about the phrase "one baptism for the remission of sins." He agrees that "heresy is defined by allegiance to the Nicene Creed," and he would add to this, he said, "to its vision of Jesus Christ. . . ." I respond to these statements below.

Kruger asks whether *The Shack* was written out of a background of perceiving God as harsh and absent. Young replies that love is the "deepest dimension of God's very being" and asks, "How can God be love . . . in essence, and do anything that does not flow from that love?" Young seems to avoid a direct answer to Kruger's question, but in chapter 28 of *Lies* ("God is One alone"), he concurs with Kruger's words.

(2) Kruger's question is whether Young agrees that "The wrath of God is God's love in action, passionately and personally opposing our destruction." Young agrees and says that God's wrath "is real, and may even be everlasting, but it belongs to His love. His wrath serves His love, His relentless affection . . . that is determined to bring us to His heart, which is our true home." Kruger adds, citing George MacDonald, that this is a "destroying affection." "The Lord's affection destroys our sin and darkness that we may be free to live in His embrace." Young answers that he wholeheartedly agrees.

(3) In light of Young's statement in *The Shack* that Jesus will travel down any road to find people, Kruger asks whether that means that "all, without exception, will be in heaven."

Young replies that he hopes so, but says that "hope is not a conclusion or a doctrine." He adds that the New Testament "leaves us with this hope," but all may not come to believe "that Jesus has embraced us all;" all may not come "to believe or to know that this is the truth." At least four times Young expresses this as his "hope."

Kruger pushes the issue further. He asks Young if all will come to the experience of knowing Jesus's embrace, so that all "without exception will . . . make their way to heaven."

Young answers that what he believes is just what he wrote in *The*

Shack: "Everyone is included" in the embrace of Jesus. While he doesn't answer Kruger directly, it seems that Young is validating that all will go to heaven.

(4) Kruger proceeds to his next question. He asks Young whether he believes that "a personal relationship with Jesus is necessary to salvation."

Young responds with "Of course." He cites his own experience in which he met the persons of the Trinity. He adds, "I am not sure what people mean by a personal relationship with Jesus," but he says that he would be dead without his encounter with Jesus. Then he adds, "Without such an encounter, we are certainly loved forever, but lost in our own darkness and pain."

(5) Kruger's fifth question is whether Young believes in hell. He notes that Young has "been there personally" in his suffering, but asks if he believes in "Eternal Conscious Torment" (ECT).

Young replies that he most definitely does not believe in this "horrendous" idea, but he thinks that hell is real, both in this life and in the next. Hell is real but "has to be understood in relationship with Jesus." Hell was created "in Jesus," and it is not "outside of Jesus." Jesus has met people in their hell and "intends to deliver us from our own evil." Young can't say how it all turns out, but he's "hopeful" in light of the reality of God's promise never to abandon his people. He trusts "Papa."

(6) Kruger's last question concerns whether Young set out to mislead or deceive people and whether he is "the antichrist."

Young replies that such a question is a "sad" one, coming mostly from Young's people. He acknowledges that *The Shack* "definitely challenges the way we in the West have been taught to believe about God." He believes Kruger's quote of Athanasius, and says that "God is good, all the time. The God I was taught was a no show in my crisis." Young affirms that when "bizarre accusations" come his way, he returns to "trusting Papa all over again, and joy sustains me."

With this, Kruger brings the interview to a close.

My Response to Young's Answers

Frankly, Young's answers hardly give any relief from the sense that Young is a consistent universalist. Also, what he doesn't say is perhaps as important as what he does say. I take up each of Young's answers to the six questions in turn.

(1) Regarding the first answer, Young and Kruger both assert that the test of orthodoxy is the Nicene Creed, and they both subscribe (almost) fully to it.

My response: The Nicene Creed (see below) is not the entire expression of orthodoxy, for additional church councils decided the crucial issues of the content of the Canon (the inspired books of the Bible), the relationship of the divine and human natures of Christ, the relationship of the persons to one another in the Trinity, and other crucial matters.

But what of the Nicene Creed? There are at least a dozen points where Young differs from its teaching. Here I cite the Creed and then show how Young differs from it.

The Nicene Creed

I believe in one God, the Father Almighty, Maker of heaven and earth, and of all things visible and invisible.

And in one Lord Jesus Christ, the only-begotten Son of God, begotten of the Father before all worlds, God of God, Light of Light, very God of very God; begotten, not made, being of one substance with the Father, by whom all things were made. Who, for us men for our salvation, came down from heaven, and was incarnate by the Holy Spirit of the virgin Mary, and was made man; and was crucified also for us under Pontius Pilate. He suffered and was buried; and the third day He rose again, according to the Scriptures; and ascended into heaven, and sits on the right hand of the Father; and He shall come again, with glory, to judge the quick and the dead; whose kingdom shall have no end.

And I believe in the Holy Ghost, the Lord and Giver of Life; who proceeds from the Father and the Son; who with the Father and the Son together is worshipped and glorified; who spoke by the prophets.

And I believe in one holy catholic and apostolic Church. I acknowledge one baptism for the remission of sins; and I look for the resurrection of the dead, and the life of the world to come. Amen.[47]

How the Creed Opposes the Beliefs of Young

a. Several terms contradict Young's idea of a "pure relation-ship" with God. As he describes it in *The Shack* and repeatedly in *Lies,* there is no subordination and no authority. There is mutual submission of all. In the Creed, note the uses of "Lord" (two times) and "Almighty" and "sits on the right hand of the Father" (a place of exaltation where no human could ever sit). Note also that the Spirit "proceeds" from the Father, indicating that the Spirit is subordinate to the Father. All of these phrases are opposed to Young's idea of relationship.

b. The use of "believe" (three to four times) contradicts Young's belief that people are already God's children whether or not they believe. Clearly, the word in this Creed suggests that some are not God's children, for they are on the outside; they do not believe. Young opposes the categories of "believers" and "unbelievers."

c. The phrase "for us men for our salvation" is clearly intended to give the purpose of Jesus's coming to save us. In his chapter 13, Young asserts that all, universally, are saved and that no one needs "to get saved." The words of the Creed assume that people are lost prior to Jesus's saving them. However, Young and UR assert that all people were created in Jesus, in God, and are never separated from him (chapters 2, 24, 27).

d. The words "was crucified also for us" affirm substitutionary penal atonement, particularly in combination with the words "for our salvation." Young has repeatedly rejected this view of the atonement. Why? Because such a view reveals God's judg-ment on Jesus Christ for our sins.

e. The words asserting that Jesus "shall come again, with glory,

---

47   http://www.trinityorc.org/creeds/

to judge both the quick [living] and the dead" no doubt refer to a judgment on people occurring after death. Romans 14:11-12 says, *"As surely as I live," says the Lord, "every knee will bow before me; every tongue will confess to God." So then, each of us will give an account of himself to God.* Second Corinthians 5:10 tells us that *we must all appear before the judgment seat of Christ, that each one may receive what is due him for the things done while in the body, whether good or bad."* All of Revelation 20 relates to judgment. Universal reconciliation and Paul Young reject such a future judgment, since all are already in God and in Christ. This idea of coming judgment is one of the most glaring differences from what UR asserts.

Note also what the Creed does not say. It does not offer an opportunity to believe after death, which contradicts what Young asserts in chapter 21, where he says that death does not end the opportunity to choose.

f. The Creed asserts that the Christian also believes in the "holy catholic [universal] and apostolic Church." These words point to both the invisible church, the Bride of Christ in which all believers are found, as well as the local institution of the church as seen in Ephesians chapters 3, 4, and 5. Young asserts that the church and other institutions are demonic and not created by God (chapter 12).

g. Finally, the Creed asserts that there is "one baptism for the remission of sins." Young says that he is not sure about this wording, but it is important to note that forgiveness of sins is something that probably offends Young. In chapter 27 of his book, Young redefines *sin* as violating a person's being rather than violating the glory or holiness of God. He also asserts that sin cannot separate anyone from God. The Creed would certainly never accept such novelty in doctrine. Additionally, Young makes no mention of the ordinances of the church: baptism and the Lord's Supper.

Both Kruger and Young say that they are willing to let the Nicene Creed be the determiner of whether they are orthodox. I've found them to be in violation of the Creed. Young doesn't "stand with the Creed;" he does not give "allegiance" to this Creed.

They should apologize for deceiving the Christian community. They are not orthodox.

(2) In regard to Kruger's second question about the nature of God's wrath, both Kruger and Young espouse UR. Typically, UR asserts that God's love limits his wrath, and this is what these revisionists are asserting. Also, to say that love destroys wrath is erroneous. The Bible says that the death of Christ propitiated, or satisfied, the wrath of God (Romans 3:26). Wrath is not destroyed, but is satisfied. If God's wrath toward sin is not satisfied, God is unjust and finally unworthy of our trust and love.

(3) In regard to the issue of whether all will go to heaven, Young's answer embraces his "hope" that this will be so. Such a "hope" is typical speech of UR. It was first used by the church father Origen, in the third century. Young says that this hope arises in the New Testament, but the Bible gives no such hope and never uses this kind of speech. Since God has spoken clearly in the Bible about who is and who is not going to heaven, it is slanderous for anyone to suggest something that challenges what God has said. Jesus said, *No one can see the kingdom of God unless he is born again* (John 3:3). In 1 John 5:12 we read, *He who has the Son has life; he who does not have the Son of God does not have life.* Young's "hope" has no more basis than wishing for gravity to disappear! In fact, it is more evil, because it rejects God's clear statements about the destiny of all.

It is interesting to note Young's words here. For after talking about "hope," he returns to his assertion that everyone is "in the embrace of Jesus" – pure UR. In *Lies* he asserts that everyone is already saved (chapter 13). See my further discussion of the vanity of such hope, above.

(4) It is surprising that Young should first answer Kruger's question about a personal relationship by saying, "of course"; but then he states that he is not sure what people mean by "a personal relationship with Jesus." Young seems to contradict himself. Either he is confused or he is subtly denying that there is such a thing. Growing up in a Christian home where his parents were missionaries, he could hardly be uncertain as to what this relationship means. He seems to be obfuscating here – obscuring what the issue is.

(Indeed, a couple hours after I wrote this paragraph, I happened to reread part of my book *Burning Down the Shack*, chapter 2, where I am citing *The Shack*, chapter 6. In my book, I say that Paul Young is correct "to affirm that a deeply personal relationship with God is essential." Who is Paul trying to mislead? Could he have forgotten over the course of ten years what he wrote about this important matter dealing with what it means to be a Christian?)

(5) His answer to the fifth question is pure UR again. He wants to redefine hell as something far less than what the Bible says. Further, his rejection in abhorrence of the idea of "eternal conscious torment" pits him against Jesus and Christian faith from the beginning till now. Jesus uses such strong language twice. When teaching his disciples about judgment, Jesus said, *Then they will go away to eternal punishment, but the righteous to eternal life* (Matthew 25:46). When Jesus told about the rich man and Lazarus, he said, *In hell, where he was in torment, he looked up and saw Abraham far away, with Lazarus by his side* (Luke 16:23).

His apostles followed suit when they spoke of *torment* and being *punished with everlasting destruction* (Revelation 14:11; 2 Thessalonians 1:8). Contrary to Young, the Bible does tell us how the future unfolds, both in heaven and in hell. Note that the Nicene Creed uses similar language: Jesus "shall come again . . . to judge." For Young to say that he "hopes" for something else is UR slander. For him to say that "hell was created in Jesus" is totally without the Bible's support. Jesus said that hell was "prepared" for the devil and his angels (Matthew 25:41). Were all these "in Jesus"?

(6) Finally, Young's answer to the sixth question shows that he thinks his writing is challenging the way "we have been taught to believe about

God." Here Young is blazing the way for his book, *Lies We Believe about God* (note the similarity in wording). He is assuming that he is the trailblazer for a new Christianity. This seems quite arrogant! His words about God being a "no show" in his time of brokenness reflect what he wrote in chapter 28.

Young, referring to "God is good, all the time," again invokes the name of Athanasius. Young expands on this phrase in *Lies* (chapter 16: "God is not good."). Young cites this church father as though Athanasius is in agreement with him, but as I show in the next appendix, this is far from the truth.

APPENDIX 2

DOES THE CHURCH FATHER ATHANASIUS SUPPORT UNIVERSAL RECONCILIATION?

The Claims of Paul Young

Both Baxter Kruger and Paul Young cite Athanasius as supporting their view of relationship with God and the nature of God as "good all the time." Indeed, Kruger has added to his website the document by Athanasius titled "The Incarnation of the Word of God."

The implication is that Athanasius supports the basic tenets of what these two believe as believers in universal reconciliation (UR) – that God is good, God is love, God doesn't judge anyone, all people are children of God, all are destined for heaven, and there is no everlasting judgment in hell.

We can all be grateful for Kruger's making known the work of Athanasius, the defender of orthodoxy. For in the search for truth, I discovered that Athanasius ends up expressing views that are totally opposed to what the basic tenets of UR and the beliefs of Kruger and Young are.

As Kruger and Young acknowledge, Athanasius of Alexandria was the premier champion of orthodoxy. Additional details about him are important. At the Council of Nicea (325), called by Constantine, the Christian emperor of Rome, Athanasius led the way to defend the eternal deity of Jesus Christ in opposition to the view of Arius, who argued that Jesus Christ had a beginning. According to Arius, Jesus was not co-eternal with the Father, nor was the Holy Spirit. Hence, there is no

Trinity. Athanasius showed that the truth of the Bible proves that the Trinity is actual and real. His view triumphed at the Council, when the vast majority of the bishops agreed with the Nicene Creed. It was later validated at another Council and has been the convinced view of the church to this day.

My Review of Athanasius's "The Incarnation of the Word of God"[48]

In the following discussion, I show that on countless doctrinal issues, Athanasius deserves the position of champion of orthodoxy and chief opponent of universalism in the past. For the present controversy over UR, Athanasius still speaks powerfully. Here is a list of the particular doctrines as I've recovered them from his "The Incarnation of the Word of God."

In this writing of Athanasius, I do not find the exact words about the goodness of God that Kruger finds. The numbers refer to the paragraphs of Athanasius's work.

Athanasius writes of the love of God (3, 15)

the goodness of God (3, 43)

and the love and goodness of God (1, 12).

He mentions the penalty of God (5).

God is not a magician (48, 50, 51, 53).

Christ is holy (14)

and distinct from the creation (17, 43).

Christ is "essential righteousness" (40).

He fully took on human nature to recreate man after the image of God (13).

He is fully God and fully human (17, 18, 19).

He pursued death (22).

The cross becomes a monument to Christ's work (24, 32).

Jesus Christ came for the purpose of dying (31)

---

48   Athanasius, "The Incarnation of the Word of God," *http://www.worldinvisible.com/library/athanasius/incarnation/incarnation.c.htm.*

to save humanity (43).

Athanasius mentions the "sign of the cross" (47, 50, 53, 55).

Christ will come again (56)

with "eternal fire" (56, 57).

There will be the recompense of judgment (38).

Christ already reigns (40).

Athanasius writes that Christ "assumed humanity that we might become God" (54). The context explains this as our being able to "perceive our unseen Father's mind" that we "might inherit immortality."

Athanasius states that the "achievements of Christ" are so numerous that they are like trying to count the waves on the open sea; they are innumerable (54).

People bear God's image and likeness (3, 4, 5, 11, 12, 13, 21, 43)

but because of the fall of Adam and Eve, the nature of all is corrupt (4, 7, 9, 41, 43, 46, 49).

People need to experience the new birth (14).

They need to be converted (27).

People would have perished under the penalty of spiritual death if Christ had not come (5, 6 [twice], 7, 8).

He writes that a man's personality penetrates his whole being (42).

All are enlightened (40).

The reality of the devil is acknowledged (25 and others);

he brought death (5).

Evil spirits are mentioned frequently (32 [four times], 45, 46, 47, 48 [often], 49, 50, 51, 52, 55 [three times]).

Athanasius places a great emphasis on the necessity to believe Christ and the gospel (15, 18, 21, 23, 24, 27, 28 [four times], 29 [three times], 30, 31 [four times], 32 [twice], 33 [the faithfulness of Jesus, twice], 35, 38, 40, 41, 50, 53, 55, 56).

Faith and obedience go together (30).

Athanasius places an even greater emphasis on the substitutionary death of Christ on behalf of all people (8, 9, 10, 16, 20, 21, 22, 25, 26, 31, 34, 37 [eight times], 38 [three times], 54).

He came to pay the debt owed for sin (20).

Christ is the Savior of all (1 [three times], 15, 25, 26, 32, 37 [three times], 38, 40 [Jesus is the ransom for all], 44, 46, 47, 49, 50, 51, 52, 53, 54, 55)

and Lord of all (34).

Athanasius cites Isaiah 53 (34 [contrasting Paul Young on child sacrifice, *Lies*, chapter 19]).

Christ fulfilled prophecy (33, 34 [about his death], 35 [about the cross]).

In light of the preceding paragraphs, it is clear that Athanasius does not support UR. Christ is the Savior of all – of all who believe.

Athanasius warns of "subordinate imposters" who mislead believers (55).

He identifies Christianity as a "religion" (1, 28, 31, 48).

He addresses how Christians are to interpret Scripture – namely, by being in fellowship with the saints (57).

He encourages the study of nature (49).

Conclusion

The preceding review of many doctrines from the work of Athanasius reveals that contemporary evangelicals believe what Athanasius believed and taught. None of these points support UR. Not one of the points that distinguishes UR, such as "the love of God limits God's justice," "there is no future judgment and no lasting hell," "all people are by nature good," and "all people are already God's children," is found in the above review.

Like Young and Kruger, those who champion UR are those who are the heretics, the "imposters" whom Athanasius identifies. They state that they want to be considered orthodox based upon their agreement with the Nicene Creed and with Athanasius, but as the above discussion of both of these sources shows, Young and Kruger are heretics and their beliefs are not orthodox.

The preceding should settle this matter!

APPENDIX 3

DOES THE ATHANASIAN CREED SUPPORT UNIVERSAL RECONCILIATION?

While the preceding appendices take up a discussion of the Nicene Creed and Athanasius and the claim of Young and Kruger that they are orthodox by these two standards, there is one more important matter. What does the Athanasian Creed say and what does it contribute to our understanding of UR? Thus, I first present the Athanasian Creed, and then I evaluate its statements in light of UR.

The Athanasian Creed is named after Athanasius, of course, but for all of its substance, it cannot be traced back to him in the fourth century. The final form copied here probably arises from the seventh century. As readers will notice, it is substantially longer than the Nicene or Apostles' Creeds.

The Athanasian Creed[49]
Whosoever will be saved, shall above all else, hold the catholic faith. Which faith, except it be kept whole and undefiled, without doubt one shall perish eternally. And the true Christian faith is this, that we worship one God in Trinity and Trinity in Unity, neither confusing the Persons nor dividing the substance.

For there is one Person of the Father, another of the Son, and another of the Holy Spirit. But the Godhead of the Father, of the Son, and of the Holy Spirit is all one, the glory equal, the majesty coeternal.

Such as the Father is, such is the Son, and such is the Holy Spirit: The Father uncreated, the Son uncreated, and the Holy Spirit uncreated; The

49   http://havasulutherans.org/catechism-explanation/creeds-confessions/.

Father infinite, the Son infinite, and the Holy Spirit infinite; The Father eternal, the Son eternal, and the Holy Spirit eternal. And yet there are not three eternals, but one eternal; just as there are not three uncreated nor three infinites, but one uncreated and one infinite.

Likewise the Father is almighty, the Son is almighty, and the Holy Spirit is almighty. And yet there are not three almighties, but one almighty. So the Father is God, the Son is God, and the Holy Spirit is God. And yet there are not three gods, but one God. Likewise the Father is Lord, the Son is Lord, and the Holy Spirit is Lord. And yet not three lords, but one Lord.

For as we are compelled by the Christian truth to acknowledge every Person by Himself to be both God and Lord, so we are forbidden by the true Christian faith to say that there are three gods or three lords.

The Father is made of none, neither created nor begotten. The Son is of the Father alone, not made nor created, but begotten. The Holy Spirit is of the Father and of the Son, neither made nor created nor begotten, but proceeding. So there is one Father, not three Fathers; one Son, not three Sons; one Holy Spirit, not three Holy Spirits.

And in this Trinity none is before or after another; none is greater or less than another; but all three Persons are coeternal together and coequal, so that in all things, as said before, the Unity in Trinity and the Trinity in Unity is to be worshiped. Whoever will be saved is compelled thus to think of the Holy Trinity.

Furthermore, it is necessary for everlasting salvation that one also believe faithfully the incarnation of our Lord Jesus Christ. For the right faith is that we believe and confess that our Lord Jesus Christ, the Son of God, is God and Man; God of the substance of the Father, begotten before the worlds; and Man of the substance of His mother, born in the world; perfect God and perfect Man, of a rational soul and human flesh subsisting. Equal to the Father as touching His Godhead and inferior to the Father as touching His manhood. Who, although He is God and Man, yet He is not two, but one Christ; One, not by changing of the Godhead into flesh, but by taking the manhood into God; One indeed, not by confusion of substance, but by oneness of Person. For just as the rational soul and flesh is one man, so God and Man is one

Christ; Who suffered for our salvation, descended into hell, rose again the third day from the dead. He ascended into heaven; He is seated at the right hand of the Father, God Almighty; from there He shall come to judge the living and the dead; at whose coming all will rise again with their bodies and will give an account of their own works. And they that have done good will enter into life everlasting; and they that have done evil into everlasting fire. This is the catholic faith; whoever does not faithfully and firmly believe this cannot be saved.

My Evaluation of How UR Violates this Creed

These are the chief points of the Athanasian Creed that universal reconciliation (UR) violates. There are eight paragraphs.

The Creed begins with the statement that one must hold or believe the "catholic [universal] faith" in order to be saved. This statement sets up the importance of what follows. It means that whoever rejects this Creed is heretical and will "perish eternally." What follows is the content of this faith.

So how does UR hold up in light of this standard? It fails on several counts; it is heresy.

To begin with, UR rejects creedal statements, as shown in a review of its history, especially its history in America. My larger book on universalism contains a whole chapter that exposes UR's rejection of creeds.

In its opening words, this Creed makes reference to "whosoever will be saved." In the seventh paragraph, these words are repeated. The final words of the Creed are that whoever doesn't believe this Creed "cannot be saved." These words, reflecting such texts as Romans 10:13 (*whoever will call on the name of the Lord will be saved*, NASB) are rejected by UR. The latter asserts that all people are already saved; no one needs "to get saved" (*Lies*, chapter 13).

Note that this Creed begins and ends with references to the everlasting judgment ("perish eternally" and "everlasting fire") that will come on those who reject the "catholic faith." Universal reconciliation rejects the idea of an everlasting hell or judgment.

The Creed emphasizes the nature of the Trinity – that all three

Persons have the same undivided substance or essence or nature. This is the "true Christian faith," but UR rejects creeds.

In the fourth and eighth paragraphs, the Persons in the Godhead are described as "Almighty." In the fifth paragraph, the title "Lord" is used of all three Persons. Note also how paragraph 2 refers to "glory" and "majesty." This type of designation is rejected in *The Shack*: "The first aspect of God is never that of the absolute Master, the Almighty. It is that of the God who puts himself on our human level and limits himself" (*The Shack,* 88). Young plays down this aspect of God's nature in all his novels.

In his books, Young writes about a "circle of relationship" involving God and people in which there is no authority and no subordination (*Lies*, chapters 7, 24, 27; *The Shack*, 122-124). Such thoughts violate this Creed.

This Creed doesn't get to the incarnation until later, and it makes a distinction regarding Jesus – that he is "begotten," and regarding the Holy Spirit – that he "proceeds" from both the Father and the Son. Thus, there are different roles within the Godhead. This suggests authority and subordination – ideas that Young rejects when he writes and talks about relationship within the Godhead.

In the eighth paragraph there is much to address. There is reference to the necessity to believe in order to have "everlasting salvation." Belief is mentioned three times, but UR asserts that people are already saved; belief is not the condition (*Lies*, chapters 13, 24). The substance of what to believe is identified as the "right faith": believing in the deity and humanity of Christ. But UR lays down no conditions of belief.

The words that Christ "suffered for our salvation" suggest penal substitution, that Christ took our place on the cross to pay the penalty that our sins demanded. Again, Young rejects penal substitution and asserts that the cross was not God's idea, but man's (*Lies*, chapters 3, 17, 19).

Finally, the Creed affirms that Jesus Christ is coming again to "judge the living and the dead." Then all "will give an account of their own works." Two destinies are given: "life everlasting" and "everlasting fire." But UR opposes all such statements. Young rejects a future judgment for anyone on the basis of their beliefs or works (*Lies*, 15, 21, 27). He asserts (erroneously citing James 2:13), that "God's mercy triumphs over God's justice because of love" (*The Shack*, 164). Because he redefines hell, there is no lasting hell or suffering. Thus, Young rejects Jesus's words recorded in Matthew 25:46 about *everlasting punishment* for some and *everlasting life* for others.

Conclusion

The Athanasian Creed is more complete and detailed than either the Apostles' Creed or the Nicene Creed. It is consistent with all the great truths found in Athanasius's "The Incarnation of the Son of God."

Another point needs to be made about what the creeds do not say. They are totally absent on such ideas that there is a chance to be saved, indeed a necessity that all will be saved, after death. They are silent on God's love limiting God's justice; that the final destiny of all people is heaven; that God loves all people the same; that all people are already God's children; that we should "hope" that all will be saved; and other UR assertions. Why is it important to recognize this absence? Because Origen, the church father, and a couple others had already begun to propound UR in the third century. Thus, Athanasius and the church in the fourth century refused to depart from the Bible and give place to any tenets of UR.

What the creeds and Athanasius do not say is as equally important as what they do say!

It is virtually beyond dispute that UR, embraced by Paul Young and Baxter Kruger, violates all of these great creeds and writings of the early church going back to the fourth century. These modern men insisted that their orthodoxy should be judged by what these creeds say and what Athanasius wrote.

By their own standard, Young and Kruger have failed! They are not orthodox. They are heterodox – heretics.

Again, the above discussion should finally settle the matter!

APPENDIX 4

THE MANY CONTRADICTIONS OF PAUL YOUNG AS A UNIVERSALIST

After reading almost all of Young's fiction and non-fiction, his blogs and articles, and his interviews, it has become apparent that there are some glaring contradictions in his reasoning and logic. While the preceding book exposes many of his contradictions to the Bible, I here outline some other contradictions.

(1) Young asserts in *Lies*, chapter 13 (118) that all people have been reconciled to God already. No one needs to "get saved" because all are already saved. He confesses "universal reconciliation" as his settled conviction. This is the primary, central teaching belonging to universal reconciliation – quite obviously! This reconciliation is attributed to God's work in Christ on the cross – that in his dying, Jesus brought all into an everlasting relationship with God.

Yet if all are already reconciled to God, why does he also say, "No, I don't believe in a doctrine that holds that every person will ultimately be reconciled full [sic] back to God. Yes, I hope that is true." He goes on, stating that he is a "hopeful Universalist. . . And in a way, who isn't?" Both of these statements derive from an article, "Does *The Shack* Teach Universalism?" found on his website (www.wmpaulyoung.com) and dated July 13, 2017.

(2) Young asserts in *Lies* (chapters 1, 24, 25) that all people are equally children of God and loved by him because all were created "in God" (*Lies*, chapters 1, 2, 7, 10, 22). Yet this again contradicts the preceding statements from his website. No person can be a child of God without

being reconciled to God. Or, putting it differently, if everyone is a child of God by virtue of creation, there is no need for anyone to be reconciled to God (the subject of *Lies*, chapter 13).

(3) Young asserts that all people are good; no one is evil, because all were created in God (who is Good) (*Lies*, chapter 2). If this is so, why then does anyone need to be reconciled to God? Why talk about being a "hopeful universalist"?

(4) Young asserts that sin does not separate anyone from God (*Lies*, chapter 27). Again, if this is so, why then talk about anyone needing to be reconciled to God, of being a "hopeful universalist"?

(5) Young asserts that hell does not separate anyone from God (*Lies*, chapter 15). Again, if this is so, why is there a need for reconciliation?

(6) If all people are good (chapter 2), and all are children of God by virtue of being created "in God" (chapters 1, 24, 25), and all are reconciled to God already (chapter 13), and sin does not separate anyone from God (chapter 27), then why talk about the cross of Christ at all – that it was man's idea that God used (chapter 17) to bring about reconciliation?

Indeed, this is the death knell of universal reconciliation; it makes the cross of Christ – his death on the cross – unnecessary.

(7) If all are already reconciled to God (chapter 13), why wrestle with the problem of death and assert that death is not more powerful than God so that he can reach through it and bring people to himself (chapter 21)? If all are already reconciled to God, all are going to heaven anyway and death is not an issue.

All the foregoing and more raise the crucial question: If people are going to reject the Bible's teaching regarding the need for people to believe in order to be reconciled to God, then why pretend to make the Bible a part of the foundation of universal reconciliation? Why bother with the Bible at all? Throughout *Lies We Believe about God*, Young gives only the slightest place to what the Bible says; and when he does cite it, he uses it in a wrongful manner, including every one of his claims about the Greek text. The chapters of my book support what I've just written.

APPENDIX 5

THREE FINAL QUESTIONS

What has led Paul Young to become a universalist?

Why do so many follow him?

What's wrong with his being a new leader?

Whether one agrees with Young's beliefs or not, I think that everyone is eager to know how he got to where he is now. It is a fair question to ask: What has led Wm. P. Young to reject his evangelical heritage (so he states in *Lies*, 236-239) and to become a universalist (confessed in *Lies*, chapter 13)?

The short answer is embedded in the question as I've stated it. Having been unsatisfied with the answers that evangelical faith gives to great questions about life, the need for salvation, and the afterlife, he embraced the answers that universal reconciliation (UR) provides. He has embraced the UR answers to such questions as: Are people who have never believed or heard the gospel lost for eternity? What is the nature of God? Can a loving God allow people to spend an eternity in judgment? If God is love, how can he also be just and holy?

Having rejected the usual Christian answers to these and other questions, he embraced an alternative solution – a solution that ultimately is anchored not in the Bible but in reason and emotion, and often contradicts the Bible.

The second question (Why do so many follow him?) needs answering, as well. I think the short answer is: In an age seeking immediate gratification, Young's teaching of universalism provides a good feeling, so that many are not willing to take the time to check to see if it accords with the truth of the Bible. The internet allows extremist and unorthodox views to spread around the world at the speed of light.

Let me give an illustration from the world of medicine about the danger that this level of communication can have.

A recent public television broadcast ("Frontline," Aug. 1, 2017) dealt with the question of whether vaccinations are worth the risk that autism or some other adverse reaction should occur among a very small percentage of children. The broadcast sought to relate the latest scientific data gathered from many countries that shows that there is no increased risk of autism from taking the triple vaccine DDR or any other vaccine, nor an increased risk of any disease from any vaccination. Instead, those parents who refuse to allow the vaccination of their children are putting their children at risk of getting serious diseases, such as measles, mumps, whooping cough, and polio. Even death may ensue. But why do parents persist in their fear of vaccinating? The number one reason given was the internet. Because of this pervasive communications tool, all kinds of personal stories are aired without critical, scientific support. Because of the social media (via Facebook, Twitter, and other platforms), people become alarmed. There is a growing distrust of the medical profession (both the doctors and the institutions), and there are a few medical quacks who agree with them.

Now here is the parallel that explains Paul Young's success. When people hear Young's stories, they find that it resonates with their own. By social media, they spread the word around the world. They usually don't consult the theological profession – their pastors or Bible school or seminary teachers – and there are a few religious quacks who agree with them. There is growing distrust of biblical truth.

There are some big names in both camps who enjoy the reputation of being "gurus" for such people. In a recent posting (July 16, 2017), Paul Young related his being interviewed by Oprah Winfrey (on July 9, 2017). He came away saying, "I want to be more like Oprah Winfrey."

But it is quite revealing what Young said during his almost hour-long interview. See it on his website, www.wmpaulyoung.com. He suggests redefining God's judgment and holiness and asserts that we are living in a time of transition where relationship (not truth, apparently) is supreme. People don't need to be "transformed" but simply need to discover who they already are.

Now let's consider the third question. What's wrong with Paul Young having his own different views of God and the Lord Jesus Christ, and to lead others to follow him? The answer is that we are not dealing with optional questions and answers about our culture, jobs and security, raising a family, and so forth. We are dealing with the eternal destiny of every human being. It is a far more serious issue than that of vaccinating for a serious or deadly disease. We're dealing with the matter of where a human being will spend eternity – a very long time, far beyond a physical life on this planet!

So we want to know the truth about the afterlife. Young has his unorthodox views, as have others. We can believe them if we wish, but at our peril. There is only one Person in the entire history of mankind who ever went through death and came back to live forever – namely Jesus Christ the Son of God, sent from heaven for the purpose of rescuing humanity from an everlasting hell. In the New Testament, the apostles recorded their witness to the life and death and resurrection of Jesus Christ. So convinced were they of what they had witnessed that all but one died as martyrs.

What credentials does Paul Young have to become an authoritative leader to contradict what Jesus and the New Testament say? Young never went through death and came back alive!

In the end, Wm. P. Young is just another unauthorized, illegitimate teacher whose views will die with him and with those who have followed him.

Meet the Author

James B. De Young, Th.D., is senior professor of New Testament Language and Literature at Western Seminary, Portland, Oregon, where he has taught NT Greek and related courses for over forty years. His training includes Moody Bible Institute (diploma), East Texas Baptist University (B.A.), Talbot Theological Seminary (B.D., Th.M.), and Dallas Theological Seminary (Th.D.). He has been a regular contributor to the Evangelical Theological Society. He has ministered abroad in Mexico, Europe, and Afghanistan. He has served at Damascus Community Church since 1971. James and his wife, Patricia Ann, live on a small farm in Damascus, Oregon. They have four children and twelve grandchildren, all living in the area.

James De Young has spent his life teaching the Bible and biblical languages. He is dedicated to empowering Christians to discern and apply biblical truth in an increasingly pluralistic culture. This has been his focus in all of his articles and various books, including those on biblical interpretation, homosexuality, Islam, women in ministry, submission to the state, and in his Burning Down the Shack. Since 2004, James has written to expose universal reconciliation as a heresy.

Contact James De Young

Email: jdey7@aol.com

Online: www.burningdowntheshackbook.com

Made in the USA
San Bernardino, CA
25 May 2020

72327541R00140